DECODING ITALIAN WINE:
A BEGINNER'S GUIDE TO ENJOYING THE GRAPES, REGIONS, PRACTICES AND CULTURE OF THE "LAND OF WINE"

By Andrew Cullen and Ryan Anthony McNally

Cover and interior design by John Yardley

TABLE OF CONTENTS

CHAPTER 1:
L'INTRODUZIONE

Have you ever puzzled over the wine list at a nice Italian restaurant, wondered what vino to pair with a pasta dish you're making for a dinner party, or contemplated what wine would go best with some pizza and a viewing of *The Godfather*?

So have we. But sorting through the Italian wine selection at a restaurant or store, complete with unfamiliar regions, grapes and classifications, can be as challenging as selecting the most picturesque area of Italy or choosing the best Fellini film.

Enter *Decoding Italian Wine: A Beginner's Guide to Enjoying the Grapes, Regions, Practices and Cultures of the "Land of Wine."* Our inspiration for a book on Italian wine has its origins in wildly varied geographic locations (Macau and Venice), movies (*The Silence of the Lambs* and *The Godfather*) and vintages (Super Tuscans and, uh, Italian table wine mixed with water). But it has one key element in common: a desire to make Italian wine more accessible to those who share our passion for good wine and Italian culture.

ANDREW'S STORY

I was at a restaurant called The Kitchen inside the Grand Lisboa casino in Macau, China, in November 2011 when I tasted one of the best wines of my life. It was my birthday, and I had just won a few hundred dollars playing roulette. The wine was the 2007 Antinori Solaia, and it was so unbelievable then I can't imagine what it will be like in 10 to 15 years as it approaches maturity. The wine had layers, depth, mouthfeel and finesse unlike anything I had ever tasted, and I'll never forget it.

This bottle instantly changed the way I looked at Italian wine, particularly Super Tuscans. I was a (self-proclaimed) French wine guru and was pulling for everyone to order a nice aged left-bank Bordeaux to pair with our Australian Wagyu steaks. But the expert sommelier at The Kitchen, which claims to house one of the largest private wine collections in the world, convinced us to go with the Solaia after we shared our food order and taste preferences with him. And I'm so happy he did.

In my previous book, *Decoding French Wine: A Beginner's Guide to Enjoying the Fruits of the French Terroir*, I mentioned a wine tasting I attended more than a decade ago with a highly astute host who was the Southeast representative for a major wine distributor. When I mentioned to him that I was gravitating toward French wines, he cheered that decision and advised I study and learn the wine regions one at a time. That way, I could submerse myself in a particular area without distraction.

Multiple trips to France and countless bottles of French wine later, I wrote *Decoding French Wine*, in which I attempted to demystify the complex world of French wines by writing in a concise, non-intimidating, fun manner so readers could absorb the content and gain a better understanding of the many amazing French wines. While I don't feel like my work is finished on that topic, I realized I wanted to do additional versions of similarly themed wine books.

That brings us to where we are now. Italy is a logical second choice for the subject matter (some would argue first choice). The only difference is that this time I wasn't bringing in decades of wine experience and multiple trips to Italy. True, I had sampled my fair share of Italian wines and reviewed many bottles for a wine website I founded called CostcoWineBlog.com. But I needed more expertise.

After sitting on the idea for almost a year, and slowly putting down those French Vacqueyras bottles I love so much in favor of Sicilian Nero d'Avola, a random conversation over lunch one day changed everything. The answer was right in front of me the whole time. We just hadn't put the pieces together yet.

RYAN'S STORY

When I was a little kid, I spent many Sundays at my maternal grandparents' home in the Greenwich Village area of New York City. Sunday dinner, which usually began mid-afternoon, was a huge part of that experience.

Dinner always consisted of some sort of Italian fare, and it was always ridiculously delicious. My grandmother, whose parents immigrated from Messina, Sicily, would cook up a huge pot of tomato sauce (we called it meat gravy) from scratch, along with a mouth-watering assortment of meats: sweet and hot Italian sausages, homemade meatballs, veal and chicken rollatini and more. These would be paired with ravioli or macaroni and, of course, crusty Italian bread.

CHAPTER 1: L'INTRODUZIONE

My grandfather was born in Chiesiola, a small Italian town about an hour from Parma. When he was 17 years old, he immigrated to the United States. After serving as a cook in the U.S. army in World War II, he returned to the States and worked for the next 40 years as a pastry chef. As you might imagine, our Sunday dinners always concluded with a vast assortment of Italian dessert items, including cannoli, seven-layer cookies, napoleons, sfogliatelle, pignoli cookies and more. During the summer, peaches soaked in red wine added some variety to the mix.

During these dinners, the adults would often enjoy a glass or two of wine. And as I grew a little older, I was allowed to have a small glass of red table wine mixed with water with my meal. In retrospect, my family's attitude toward this light consumption mirrored that of many parents in Italy, where it's not unusual for minors to have a little wine during family meals.

A decade or so later, while I was in college at Wake Forest, I spent a semester abroad in Venice, Italy. Living on the Grand Canal was an unforgettable experience, and part of my cultural immersion involved sampling Italian wine. Of course, I was on a college budget, so many of my wine purchase decisions were driven by price rather than quality. At a dollar or two a pop, I even indulged in a few boxes of wine (oh, the horror).

Still, given the course of an entire semester, I was bound to learn something beyond how to order a liter of house wine in Italian — *Vorrei un litro di vino della casa, per favore* — though that was a nice ancillary benefit (see Appendix II for more helpful Italian phrases).

I started to learn a little about the regions and grapes of Italy, how they differed and how certain areas had their own quirky specialties. Venice, for example, had a wine called Fragolino that boasted unusual hints of strawberry. Cinque Terre, a group of five small coastal towns, was known for Sciacchetra, a tasty sweet white wine. And so on.

In the years that followed, I made two return trips to Italy and attempted to continue my Italian cultural education whenever I got the chance. I started to dig into Italian films, watching the movies of Federico Fellini, Roberto Rossellini, Vittorio De Sica and many others, eventually launching a website, VivaItalianMovies.com, dedicated to Italian cinema. I continued to sample new Italian wines. And I fruitlessly endeavored to keep my Italian from getting rusty.

Some pursuits went better than others. I discovered that getting my electric oven hot enough to cook the perfect Neapolitan pizza was difficult to do without burning the house down.

One day I found myself at lunch with my friend Andrew, talking about my Italian movies website, my experience studying abroad and our mutual love for Italian wine.

"I like to drink wine more than I used to."

— Don Vito Corleone, *The Godfather*

This book had to be done — and not just because we needed an excuse to drink copious amounts of fine Italian wine. No, we wanted to approach Italian wine in a way that hadn't been done before.

Simply put, learning about Italian wine can be more intimidating than a Clint Eastwood glare in one of Sergio Leone's spaghetti westerns. It's a massive study with more than 2,000 grape varieties planted across more than a million active vineyards all over the country.

Our objective isn't to cover all these areas. There are books that do that, and if you're that advanced in your wine studies, you probably know what those books are. (We recommend *The Sotheby's Wine Encyclopedia*.)

But for the everyday wine lover who wants to better understand the grapes, winemaking practices, regions and world-class nature of Italian wine, this book is for you. We're going to cover a lot, but we're going to do it in a fun, laid-back, non-academic way.

"A census taker once tried to test me. I ate his liver with some fava beans and a nice Chianti."

— Hannibal Lecter, *The Silence of the Lambs*

That means keeping it light and loose, with pop culture references and fun factoids about Italian wine mixed in with easy-to-digest information about Italy's wine regions and grapes.

Our goal is for you to be able to open a wine list at an Italian restaurant and know what to expect from most of the bottles on the menu, so you can pair them with your meal.

We want you to walk into a wine shop, go to the Italian section, scan down to Piedmont, and pick out a nice Barbera d'Asti to take to your friend's house for dinner so you can discuss the blueberry, dark cherry, vanilla and toasted oak flavors of the wine and how they perfectly complement the meal.

We're not going to cover the small, obscure wines that grow in tiny areas of the Italian landscape because you're not likely to see them in your wine shop or local restaurant — and because we secretly envy anyone who has access to these tasty rarities. If you travel to Italy, though, we highly recommend you focus on these seldom-exported wines.

And make no mistake, there is plenty of unique vino to be had in the country the ancient Greeks referred to as "Oenotria" — the land of wine. In fact, wine has been a vital part of culture and cuisine in Italy for thousands of years. The mega-popular wine regions we know today such as Barolo or Brunello were actually mega-popular 4,000 years ago. When the Greeks came over to settle much of the southern part of Italy, they marveled at how grapes grew so easily there, the soil, weather and geography perfect for their cultivation.

This also proved to be the staging ground for what we know today as "viticulture," or the process and system of making wine, due to their early experimentation with bottling and barrel aging. These roots led to wine being an integral part of Italian life from the very beginning, through the Roman Empire and up through today.

"I regard those as wise who employ old wine freely and study old stories."

— Plautus (Titus Maccius Plautus), Roman playwright, 254-184 B.C.

During the 19th century, advances in winemaking and bottling enabled Italians to more easily export wine. This resulted not only in Italian wine becoming much more readily available in the United States (*molto buono!*), but also in the complete befuddlement of Americans as they tried to decipher the strange Italian wine labels (*molto brutto!*).

Take your basic garden-variety/incredibly delicious Sangiovese, for example. The typical label doesn't just come out and say the wine is made with Sangiovese, and even if it did, Sangiovese is only beginning to become a familiar grape to many early-stage wine drinkers in the United States. Most people understand Italian wines from their region such as Chianti, not even knowing the wine is comprised predominantly of Sangiovese grapes.

On top of that, there are multiple levels of wine classifications, as well as the related rogue movement that spawned the Super Tuscan trend and led to some of the best wines in the world coming out of Italy, such as the aforementioned Solaia.

As is the case with most European wines, building a strong understanding of what's in the bottle relies heavily on geography. In the United States, you might find Cabernet Sauvignon from Washington state, all areas of California, Arizona, New York, Virginia and Oregon.

But in Italy you'll find that most grapes are isolated to a certain region, or sometimes regions, where the soil and weather are optimal for cultivating that particular grape. Take Corvina, for instance. This awesome light-red grape is primarily grown in the Veneto region of Italy, and you'll find it in classic Italian wines such as Valpolicella and Amarone. But the label will simply specify the region.

In 1963, with the introduction of DOC (Denominazione di Origine Controllata), Italy sought to regulate grape cultivation across the country to bring an extra level of quality assurance for customers. These regulations have expanded over time, and we'll cover them in more detail in Chapter 5.

Our hope is that, at the completion of this book, you'll have an understanding of which grapes grow in which regions and how the various regions' winemaking practices impact the final product you consume. And more importantly, the next time you're trying to figure out what bottle of Italian wine to purchase, you'll have the confidence and knowledge to have fun with the process and select the bottle that best enhances the occasion. *Salute!*

CHAPTER 2:
ITALIAN WINE AND CULTURE

When Ryan was studying abroad in Venice, he made an amazing discovery when he ventured out to eat: a carafe of the house wine was often no more expensive than a bottle of water — and occasionally less so.

His first thought: This is the greatest country in the world! His second: Can I subsist for an entire semester on a diet of wine, bread and pizza?

But after a while, much like grapes fermenting in a barrel, bigger multicultural lessons soaked in. Such as: For Italians, wine is as much a part of a meal as water.

It makes sense given the country's history with wine, dating back thousands of years to the ancient Etruscans and Romans. While the viticulture has had its ups and downs in recent centuries, Italian wine production and culture has flourished during the last 50-plus years.

It's true that wine consumption in Italy has decreased a bit in recent times, with factors such as the economic downturn and an increase in Italian craft beers contributing to the shift.

But wine remains a steady presence in Italian life. Consider: The average Italian drinks between 0.6 gallons and 13.6 gallons per year (figures vary based on source), compared to roughly 2.7 gallons per year per U.S. citizen.

So it's still a big part of the culture and an integral part of meals and life. And given that Italians have been at this wine stuff a few millennia longer than us here in North America, it stands to reason they might be able to teach us a couple things about vino. Here are four quick takeaways from Italian wine culture you'd be wise to heed:

1) **Don't save wine for special occasions.** Drinking a little vino doesn't have to be a big, fussy spectacle. That's not to say you shouldn't break out a pricy bottle of Barolo or a fancy Super Tuscan for a big celebration. But think of wine as a sustaining, stimulating beverage that's part of a balanced lifestyle.

2) **Sip slowly and avoid excess.** In Italy there's a tradition of "slow food," with residents savoring the food and meals often extending for hours. (Check out Chapter 11 for more on Italian food and wine.) Yet despite the long meals and the prevalence of wine, moderation is the rule when it comes to consumption.

3) **Look beyond the big names.** It seems like behind every Italian piazza lies a hidden local wine treasure, and many Italians partake of these local producers. While finding these small hidden gems stateside is a challenge since most aren't distributed beyond Italy's borders, we encourage you to take a more adventurous approach to your Italian wine tasting, seeking out new and more obscure vintages rather than just sticking with the same 'ol bottle of Chianti.

4) Keep it simple. Yes, learning about the aromas and tastes in your glass of Italian wine is part of the learning experience, but that doesn't mean you have to make a showy spectacle of sniffing, swirling and swishing. Consuming wine is also about enjoying the simplicity of the beverage, this nectar of the gods created from fermented grapes.

This lack of pretense is apparent in the glassware Italian restaurants use to serve wine, which can range from the fanciest of stemware to the most modest of water or juice glasses. In our experience, most wines taste equally good regardless of drinking receptacle.

In fact, some of the best meals we've had in Italy consisted of nothing more than an exquisite prosciutto and mozzarella panini, the flavors mingling to perfect effect, paired with a glass of the house red wine.

FAST FACT

In the 1970s, the average Italian drank an impressive 29 gallons of wine per year. *Forte!*

CHAPTER 3:
MAP OF ITALIAN
WINE REGIONS

Valle d'Aosta

Piedmont

Lombardia

Trentino-Alto Adige

Veneto

Friuli-Venezia Giulia

Liguria

Emilia-Romagna

Tuscany

Marche

Umbria

Lazio

Abruzzo

Molise

Puglia

Campania

Basilicata

Sardinia

Calabria

Sicily

CHAPTER 4:
PRIMARY ITALIAN GRAPE VARIETALS

"Chi ha pane e vino, sta meglio del suo vicino."
("Who has bread and wine is better off than his neighbor.")

– Italian proverb

One of the pleasures of enjoying Italian wine is experiencing the different grape varietals indigenous to Italy. But this seemingly complicated study can also be frustrating to many early-stage wine consumers who find the grape varietals less familiar (and harder to pronounce) than more commonplace grapes like Cabernet Sauvignon, Syrah and Merlot.

We understand. In our fledgling wine years, we stuck with the Merlots and Cabernets of the world (when we weren't indulging in the Mad Dogs and Boone's Farms). But take it from our experience: You'll be doing yourself a major disservice by not sampling the different varietals that call Italy home, and many times you'll find grapes that match your preferences and even exceed your expectations.

As you've probably gathered, picking out Italian wine is more involved than simply grabbing any old Chardonnay off the shelf. It's a combination of geography and experience — the ability to match the grapes and the regions you like the most.

As we mentioned earlier in this book, we're not going to look at every single grape varietal that's grown in Italy. Instead, we're going to focus on the ones you'll see most often at your local wine shop and on restaurant wine lists. Let's start by taking a look at some of the top red grapes of Italy.

THE KEY RED GRAPE VARIETALS OF ITALY

SANGIOVESE

Sangiovese (pronounced "san-joe-vay-say") is the powerhouse red grape of Italy and the varietal you'll find in many of Italy's most popular and world-class wines, including those from Chianti, Nobile di Montepulciano and Brunello. Sangiovese is planted heavily in Tuscany, where it's frequently blended with Cabernet Sauvignon and Merlot to create the "Super Tuscan" wines mentioned earlier, as well as the Umbria region.

Bettino Ricasoli, also known as the "Iron Baron," was a 19th century Italian politician and eventual prime minister who's credited with having invented the original recipe for Chianti. The formula was a Sangiovese blend with two white grapes (Malvasia and Trebbiano) that was to become Chianti Classico. Most of the Chiantis produced today have little or no white grapes blended in them.

Sangiovese, like many of the Italian grape varietals we'll cover, has characteristics that can differ based on the terroir (soil and growing conditions) and winemaking techniques of different regions throughout Italy. In general, though, expect Sangiovese to be medium in body (although it can go slightly lighter or fuller) with tight tannins and flavors of dried red fruit, cherries and plum.

NEBBIOLO

Nebbiolo ("neb-ee-oh-lo") is one of the most prestigious varieties in Italy and is best known for its role as the foundation of high-end wines such as Barolo and Barbaresco. One of the first varieties to bud, it's also one of the last to mature.

The skin of the Nebbiolo is very thin and the grape has a low color pigmentation, so a long maceration process is required to make wines from Nebbiolo. This contributes to the acidity and tannins Nebbiolo-based wines are known for and is also part of the reason these wines benefit from aging.

Nebbiolo yields garnet-colored, full-bodied wines with lots of complexity and flavors — dark fruits and berries, spices and herbs, and

"Nebbia" is the Italian word for fog. Since Nebbiolo grapes are primarily grown in the Piedmont region among the foothills of the western Alps, an area that's prone to fog — particularly in fall as these berries are ripening — many have speculated this is the source of the grape's name.

leather. It may not be ideal for beginners, but it's a must as you get deeper into your wine journey.

BARBERA

Barbera ("bar-bear-ah") is grown in the world-class area of Piedmont, most commonly around the towns of Asti and Alba, hence the popular wines Barbera d'Asti and Barbera d'Alba. For a long time, Barbera held the crown as the king of Italy's red wine grapes, but Sangiovese has overtaken it in terms of popularity in the last couple decades.

Barbera is going to be more of a spicy drink, medium in body with fewer tannins but a fair amount of acidity. Flavors will be red and black berry fruit, and the wines overall will tend to be bright and juicy. They are excellent values and pair well with traditional Italian dishes as well as pizza.

CORVINA

Corvina ("core-vee-nah") is a key grape in popular wines like Amarone and Valpolicella from the Veneto region, two heavy hitters that must be properly explored as part of your Italian wine journey. Amarone wines are some of the highest end in Italy and are capable of aging for several decades. They can get expensive, but it's hard to argue they aren't worth the price. Valpolicella is also highly regarded but available at price points that are much more accessible.

Corvina is generally a little lighter in body and color than some of the other richer reds. It's easy-drinking with abundant red fruit and dark cherry flavors. Corvina's high acidity can also bring a touch of sour cherry flavor.

MONTEPULCIANO

Montepulciano ("mon-tay-pul-chee-ah-no") is an excellent grape varietal to put in your back pocket of knowledge. You can serve it with a wide variety of food, it will please most crowds and it's rather inexpensive. Montepulciano d'Abruzzo is a popular Montepulciano wine, and we've tasted several bottles between $8 and $15 that were outstanding for the money.

Montepulciano exhibits a little smoke and tobacco scent, while being silky in the mouth with flavors of red fruit and plum.

FAST FACT

The grape varietal Montepulciano is easily confused with the Tuscan town of the same name that produces the popular Vino Nobile di Montepulciano and Rosso di Montepulciano, which consist primarily of Sangiovese. We'll be covering these wines soon.

DOLCETTO

The word *dolcetto* literally means "little sweet one," and it's not clear what that has to do with the wine name, but some guess it's because Dolcetto ("dole-chet-oh") can be easier to grow than other varietals. The name certainly doesn't have much to do with its taste.

Dolcetto can be a little spicy with low acidity, meaning it's better to drink young. The flavors of Dolcetto are generally blueberry, blackberry and black licorice. Frequently priced between $10 and $15, Dolcetto wines offer a lot of deliciousness for the buck.

AGLIANICO

Aglianico ("ag-lee-on-ee-coh"), a popular varietal in the Campania and Basilicata regions in Southern Italy, is a big, strong grape, built to age. It's dark in the glass with a full body and heavy tannic structure leading to a muscular, rustic mouthfeel. Aglianico wines are best enjoyed after they've laid down for a few years, preferably with a hearty meal.

PRIMITIVO

Primitivo ("prim-ee-tee-vo"), a key grape in Southern Italy, is likely the most familiar of the varietals we're highlighting here because it's genetically equivalent to Zinfandel in the United States.

It's usually full in body (although it can sometimes be lighter), with fruit flavors of blackberry, violets and spicy pepper notes.

FAST FACT

Primitivo originated in Croatia, where it's known as Crljenak Kaštelanski.

NERO D'AVOLA

Nero d'Avola ("Nare-oh dav-oh-la"), which means "Black Grape of Avola," is almost the Malbec of Italy in terms of its growing popularity. A few years ago you might be lucky to see one or two bottles on store shelves, but today many shops are offering a wider selection. It's grown primarily in Sicily and is used to produce high-quality wines that can frequently be found at reasonable prices.

Nero d'Avola is usually dark on the pour, fairly full in body, with very noted herbal scents and a peppery finish. It is, like so many Italian red wines, perfect for food pairing but equally capable of standing on its own.

THE KEY WHITE GRAPE VARIETALS OF ITALY

ARNEIS

Arneis ("are-nayz") is an excellent white grape to start off with. It's generally floral on the nose, sometimes with scents of honey. It has decent body to it and exudes ripe fruit, apple, pear and peach flavors.

Arneis is grown primarily in the Piedmont region, where many of the country's powerhouse red wines (such as Barolo and Barbaresco) are also produced. For that reason, it's sometimes referred to as "Barolo Bianco," which is a nod both to its quality and the finicky nature of its growth. Arneis literally means "little rascal" because the grape ripens late and is susceptible to rot.

Roero is a top area known for producing world-class Arneis, and many of the excellent whites coming out of Roero are starting to gain a larger following outside of Italy. Years ago Arneis was thought of as a blending element for bigger red wines to help add complexity and depth (a similar technique is used in Australian and northern French Rhone wines), but today's Arneis wines possess the finesse, elegance and body to stand on their own.

Arneis is offered from a handful of California producers, such as Jacuzzi vineyards, which specialize in a range of different Italian varietals grown in Sonoma County. We've found Jacuzzi wines to be very good, and their tasting room is free, making it a must-stop winery on any trip through Sonoma.

PINOT GRIGIO

Everyone seems to have their opinions when they talk about Pinot Grigio ("peeh-no gree-jo"), and many aren't favorable, largely due to the bland and boring connotations wine drinkers tend to have with the varietal. But Pinot Grigio (or Pinot Gris as it's known in other parts of the world) varies in character significantly depending on where it's grown. And Italian Pinot Grigio is known as some of the best in the world, especially when you explore regions such as Alto Adige and Friuli-Venezia Giulia where Pinot Grigio thrives.

Italian Pinot Grigio is usually crisp and light, with subtle citrus flavor and mild floral notes. Sometimes these wines can be drier than Pinot Grigio from other parts of the world. We find them to be very food-friendly, particularly for starters or lighter fare, including a lot of salads, chicken, pork and white fish dishes.

There are three regions where you'll commonly find good Italian Pinot Grigio:

Trentino-Alto Adige

Located in the northernmost part of Italy, Alto Adige borders Austria and Switzerland. The wines from Alto Adige are minerally with natural acidity, resulting in a bit more of a complex Pinot Grigio, and one favored by many white wine fans in the know.

Friuli-Venezia Giulia

Pinot Grigio from Friuli-Venezia Giulia, located in the northeastern part of the country, is right on par with Alto Adige. It's full-bodied and noticeably heavier in the mouth than the lighter style from other regions, and it possesses strong apple, apricot and peach flavors with a good dose of acidity.

Lombardy

Lombardy is a smaller player in the Pinot Grigio scene but a growing wine region overall that's known not only for a lot of different white varietals, but also for its sparkling wines and top-notch reds.

VERDICCHIO

Verdicchio wine ("ver-deek-kee-oh") is made from the grape of the same name, and it's rising in popularity around the United States. Grown primarily in the Marche region of east-central Italy, it's often confused with Trebbiano, both in taste and in the vineyards themselves, and it's easy to understand why since they share many characteristics.

Verdicchio bottles can be scored for a pretty good price (frequently $10 to $20). Case in point: We enjoyed a beautiful $16 Verdicchio before writing this section (the 2012 Fontezoppa Verdicchio, if you're curious). Like many Verdicchios, it had a somewhat muted nose but developed on the palate with strong acidity and flavors of citrus, lemon and lime.

These wines are excellent picks when you're looking for something a little bit different. Plus, they pair well with food. You owe it to yourself to try some of these wines as part of your Italian wine journey. We think you'll get hooked.

MOSCATO (MUSCAT)

"It's a celebration / clap clap bravo / lobster and shrimp / and a glass of Moscato"

– Drake, "Do It Now"

If Arneis and Verdicchio are just beginning to grow in popularity outside of Italy, then Moscato ("mos-cot-oh") is the grape that's been blazing a path for them the past few years. Moscato, or Muscat as it's commonly known, has seen an atmospheric rise in popularity lately, driven in part by the hip-hop community, which can elevate products to mass audiences with a single tweet or photo. In some hip-hop circles, Moscato has become the new Cristal.

Moscato is grown primarily in Piedmont and is used to make Moscato d'Asti, a semi-sweet, semi-sparkling wine that's found a loyal following in the United States. It's generally pretty inexpensive, low in alcohol and an interesting alternative to the regular white wines many consumers find too familiar or boring.

It's a distinctive grape with notable fragrance and flavors of citrus, lemon and stone fruit. Moscato is used to make many different wines, even brandies and sweet dessert wines. Like Prosecco sparkling wines, it can be a great aperitif or digestif.

A likely reason Moscato d'Asti has taken off is because it's designed to be fun. You can drink it first thing in the morning (if that's your gig) or late at night, and the slight fizziness combined with the low alcohol make it something to enjoy and talk about with friends. It's a versatile wine that's frequently priced less than $20, with some bottles less than $10. Next time you're looking for something a little different to take to a dinner party, try bringing a Moscato d'Asti along and see how it goes over.

GARGANEGA

Garganega (gar-gah-neh-gah) is the primary grape used to make Soave wine, which is another outstanding white wine value in Italy. Soave wines must be comprised of at least 70 percent Garganega. We'll cover Soave in more detail in the "Veneto" section of Chapter 6, but you can expect wines made from Garganega to be light to medium in body and pretty dry, with citrus flavors and often almond and vanilla notes on the finish.

TREBBIANO

It's the second most widely planted grape in the world and is used in more than a quarter of Italy's DOC wines, yet Trebbiano ("treb-ee-ah-no") flies under the radar. The reason? It's most commonly employed as a blending component, and its moniker rarely appears on labels.

FAST FACT

Trebbiano grapes are also used to produce balsamic vinegar. During the course of aging and fermentation over many years, the Trebbiano grape juice syrup gradually turns its trademark dark brown color and develops the unique balsamic vinegar flavor loved by many.

In a few notable cases, though, the Trebbiano grape is the foundation for wines that are pleasantly fresh and fruity with the right amount of acidity to balance everything out. Popular examples include Umbria's Orvieto wines and Abruzzo's Trebbiano d'Abruzzo, both available at very reasonable prices.

VERMENTINO

You don't have to be on island time to enjoy Vermentino ("ver-men-tee-no"), but its origins and crisp acidity make it perfect for pairing with seafood, oysters and calamari, regardless of whether you're dining oceanfront or sipping a glass in more humble surroundings.

Grown primarily in Sardinia, the large island in the Mediterranean west of the Italian coastline, Vermentino is a white wine varietal that's gaining in popularity with restaurant insiders and consumers in the know. Newer plantings are emerging on the Italian mainland in parts of Tuscany, Piedmont and Umbria, and you'll also find bottles hailing from Corsica Island.

Vermentino wines are clean, dry, light in color and packed with tangy acidity. The wines offer citrus fruit with lemon and orange notes, sometimes more nut and almond flavor, and generally exude a good deal of mineral and stoniness on the finish.

With many Vermentino bottles priced in the $10 to $15 range, we highly recommend working this scrumptious varietal into your white wine rotation.

AN ONGOING JOURNEY

There are several hundred grape varietals planted throughout Italy, and we've covered 16 of the more common ones you'll see. In the course of your wine studies, you'll likely run across many more, and we encourage you to try as many as you can. You never know what small-production grape varietal will become the next big thing.

CHAPTER 5:
ITALIAN WINE
CLASSIFICATIONS

Understanding the complex world of Italian wine classifications is no easy task, but it's essential to reading label and bottle markings and knowing how they relate to the end product. Just keep in mind that, like most classification systems, the Italian wine version has its limitations.

Italian wine classification became official in 1963 with the introduction of DOC, Denominazione di Origine Controllata ("Controlled designation of origin"), aimed at providing a certain level of quality assurance for wines, as well as cheeses. The idea was that products produced in a specific region used approved and recognized practices from that region. As a result, consumers would ultimately be more informed about what they were purchasing.

At that time there were three levels of designation, all of which remain today:

- *Vino da Tavola, or VdT* (table wine): basic wine level, labels may not even include vintage or estate name (similar to vin de table in France)

- *Denominazione di Origine Controllata* (controlled designation of origin) *or DOC:* this wine is produced in a defined winemaking region of Italy using traditional practices from that region.
- *Denominazione di Origine Controllata e Garantita* (controlled designation of origin guaranteed) *or DOCG:* same as above, but with slightly more stringent guidelines

The third level, DOCG (with the addition of "guaranteed" language), was special because government officials would actually taste the final wines. If they passed the taste test, a band would be affixed around the bottle's neck to signify approval and prevent anyone from tampering with the wine once it achieved its designation. You will see this band on many top-tier Italian wines today.

THE RISE OF THE SUPER TUSCANS

The simple three-level DOC system immediately met with controversy, especially in light of an early rogue wine movement that eventually led to what's known as Super Tuscans.

Under traditional DOC rules for the Chianti region, for example, wines could be no more than 70 percent Sangiovese and had to include at least 10 percent of white. But the limitations of these guidelines became apparent in the early '70s when Tuscan winemakers began creating remarkable wines that didn't fit within these parameters, such as Tenuta San Guido's 1972 Sassicaia. That wine, comprised of 90 percent Cabernet Sauvignon and 10 percent Cabernet Franc, won an international tasting of Cabernets.

The disconnect between the quality of these wines and their "vino da tavola" label led the Italian government to revise the system and introduce the IGT category to help remedy this classification shortcoming — albeit just a little.

IGT (INDICAZIONE GEOGRAFICA TIPICA)

IGT was introduced in 1992 as a new second level in the classification system and a home for wine producers who worked outside the DOC parameters, such as the Super Tuscan wine manufacturers.

Technically, IGT wines fall above the "vino da tavola" table wine category but below the official DOC and DOCG levels, but again this classification is best viewed as a loose guide. In many cases the ranking system may hold true, but for the premium IGT wines that are on par with the top Bordeaux names over in France, not so much. (Note: A few Super Tuscans have now been given DOC or DOCG classifications.)

THREE OTHER CLASSIFYING TERMS TO NOTE

The Italian legislature has approved the use of several other terms to designate the quality or winemaking practices of the wines of Italy. These three are important to note in your studies on how to decode Italian wine:

Classico

Classico refers to wines that adhere to strict historical winemaking practices for that defined region. Valpolicella Classico is an example of how a bottle may be designated – Valpolicella is the region, and Classico is its "quality" classification, meaning these wines are generally a little more premium than a wine that doesn't include the Classico mark.

Chianti Classico is a popular one you'll see at stores and on restaurant wine lists. This one is a little different and a bit confusing, since Chianti Classico is actually a region inside of Chianti. It's generally considered a little more premium than standard Chianti, and it must contain an alcohol level of at least 12 percent.

Superiore

When you see Superiore on an Italian wine label, it usually means the wine has a slightly higher alcohol level and has been aged longer at the winery.

Riserva

Riserva wines also typically have higher alcohol levels, and they must be aged for a designated amount of time at the winery. This time varies between regions and can be as little as three years for Chianti Riserva, or up to five years for Barolo and Brunello.

THE BOTTOM LINE ON ITALIAN WINE CLASSIFICATIONS

Italian wine classifications can be a helpful starting point when choosing a bottle, but they're not the be-all-end-all. Consider that within the DOC category, for example, you'll find dozens of bottles ranging from $5 to $50 and beyond, and the quality of these wines can vary as much as the price point.

As you embark on your Italian wine studies, try different classifications of wine in addition to sampling new grapes and bottles from various regions. Use the classification system and quality designators as a way to hone in on the characteristics of certain wines, to better understand their similarities and differences.

This will not only broaden your understanding of the vast world of Italian wine but will also help you determine which wines you prefer, which is ultimately the most important thing in your wine journey.

CHAPTER 6:
PRIMARY ITALIAN WINE-GROWING REGIONS

Now you're ready for the big one: learning about the top wine regions in Italy. By combining the information you've acquired thus far with a little geographical knowledge, you'll build a greater appreciation for the methods, characteristics and traditions that go into each bottle you enjoy. And you'll be able to select a wine with greater confidence and insight.

So as a tribute to all Italy offers, let's take a deeper dive into the specific regions and look at what types of wines are made where. Bring your geography hat (preferably a fedora), and get ready to learn how to decode Italian wine.

MANY DIFFERENT MICROCLIMATES, MANY DIFFERENT STYLES OF WINE

"When Santa visits his paisans,
With Dominic he'll be.
Because the reindeer cannot climb
The hills of Italy."

— Lou Monte, "Dominic the Donkey"

Italy has 20 different wine regions, and with their proximity to the Alps and the constant rolling hills, the country offers many different microclimates for growing all the grapes we've mentioned.

As anyone who has traveled across Italy via train can attest, the broad, diverse landscape is frequently stunning. The small growing areas and pockets of beauty throughout the country are part of what makes Italy, and many other European locales, such a prize in the wine community.

One simple trick we've picked up is to Google the specific region of the wine(s) you're consuming. It helps to just read a quick primer on the landscape, the climate and the local culture, and if you're as addicted to mobile devices as we are, your smartphone or tablet is close by at all times.

It also helps to have an idea where these areas fall on the map. This way you can begin to determine which areas of the country produce the wines you like best, and you can dig further into the smaller surrounding areas to find some real gems.

As we've done in previous chapters, our discussion of wine regions will stay within the bounds of what the average wine consumer will find in his or her local wine shop and on the typical wine list at Italian restaurants. Should you make your pursuit of Italian wines a lifetime journey – and we hope you do – we highly recommend sampling from all the smaller ones as well.

That said, let's begin in Piedmont, home to some of the best wine in the world, where you can find two of the three "Killer B's" of Italian wine — Barolo and Barbaresco. (Brunello, the third "B," will follow in the Tuscany section.)

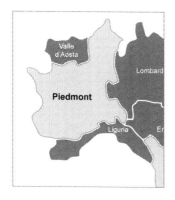

PIEDMONT (PIEMONTE)

Piedmont is located in the northwest corner of Italy. You may be familiar with it from the 2006 Winter Olympic Games, which were held in Turin, the capital of Piedmont.

Many midsize to large wine shops will feature a subsection of Piedmont wines within their Italian wine display. (This is common with Tuscan wines as well.) Make it a point to frequent stores that organize their selection in such a way, as it indicates an appreciation for the breadth of wine from each country.

Piedmont commands its own section because, like Bordeaux in France, it produces many of Italy's world-recognized wines, including the aforementioned Barolo and Barbaresco as well as Barbera, Dolcetto and Nebbiolo.

The main grapes grown in Piedmont (following suit) are Nebbiolo, Barbera and Dolcetto, and you'll see that sometimes the name of the wine will carry the grape or region on its label. (Note: Barbera and Dolcetto are covered more extensively in Chapter 4.)

FAST FACT

Piedmont is also home to the Vermouth spirit, which was first produced in the area in the mid-18th century.

Barolo

Barolo ("bah-roe-loe") is a small area, just over 30 square miles, which produces some of the most intense, complex and tannic red wines in the country. They are beautiful expressions of the Nebbiolo grape and are heavy hitters that don't reach their full potential until they've had a good eight to 12 years of maturation in the bottle.

Barolo wines are incredibly food-friendly when paired with the right meal, usually something substantial such as red meat that can stand up to the power of the wine. Barolo wines are not inexpensive, but with their higher price tag comes a premium wine experience.

Barbaresco

Barbaresco ("bar-bah-ress-coh") is another super-small wine zone that's tucked next door to Barolo, but Barbaresco wines are a little different than their neighboring Barolos even though they both consist of the same Nebbiolo grape.

Barbaresco benefits from its proximity to the Tanaro River, which runs through the region and creates a slightly different microclimate than Barolo. As a result, wines from Barbaresco tend to be less tannic, making them ready to enjoy at a younger age than the wines of Barolo.

World-class wines such as these can command a premium, and one attribute Barbaresco wines share with Barolos is their steep price tag, usually starting in the $40 range and running as high as several hundred dollars.

The Nebbiolo grape is particularly finicky to grow, much like Pinot Noir in the Burgundy region of France. As a result, the yields can sometimes be lower depending on weather conditions and other variables, and the prices will adjust accordingly.

This is where generational winemaking expertise comes into play. Many of the deeply rooted winemakers benefit from decades of experience farming these grapes. In the hands of these expert Italian winemakers, Nebbiolo grapes have been producing excellent wines for many years, and their reputation precedes them.

Gavi

Gavi ("gah-vee") is a fantastic and highly praised white wine produced in the Piedmont region from the Cortese grape. These wines are fruity, dry and light with crisp acidity. Flavors are typically lemon, lime, green apple and pear. Gavi achieved DOCG status in 1998.

We'd read that many locals find the wine pairs nicely with seafood, so we decided to give it a shot. We purchased the (widely available) 2013 Mauro Sebaste Gavi and paired it with fresh Copper River salmon (white fish may be even better), with just a light garlic olive oil and lemon glaze on it. It was phenomenal, and a pairing we'll be enjoying more in the future.

Bottom line: White wine fans would be doing themselves an injustice to ignore Gavi. Many bottles run between $15 and $20, and you'd be hard pressed to find similarly priced whites that taste better.

Moscato d'Asti

Produced in Asti from the Moscato grape — as the label in this case clearly indicates — Moscato d'Asti ("mos-cot-oh dahss-tee" is an enormously popular white entry in the (slightly) sparkling wine category. For more, see the "Moscato" section in Chapter 4.

Asti Spumante

Asti Spumante ("ah-stee spoo-mahn-tay") is also made from Moscato and has similar characteristics while being drier and more on the sparkling side with a higher alcohol content – typically edging closer to 10 percent compared to about 5 percent alcohol for a Moscato.

VENETO

As the home of Venice, the region of Veneto holds a special place in our hearts, and it's also one of our go-to areas for high-quality, competitively priced wines. It edges up on the Alp foothills in northeastern Italy, so it's largely a hilly landscape with a rather temperate climate.

The main wine areas of Veneto are Valpolicella, Bardolino and Soave, and the region's key wines range from the popular bubbly Prosecco to the world-class red wine Amarone.

Valpolicella

Valpolicella ("val-pole-ee-chel-la") is one of those wines many beginners might not gravitate to because of the lack of description on the label. While Valpolicella wines are typically made from three varietals — Corvina, Rondinella and Molinara — the labels often offer little more than short terminology such as Valpolicella Classico or Valpolicella Superiore (a slight step up). They are easy-drinking, flavorful wines made for those in the "know" — a.k.a. those wise enough to read this book.

Valpolicella wines (particularly the ones we see imported in the United States) are usually robust, full-bodied big reds, almost "baby Amarones" that can be scored for half or a third the price of an Amarone. In fact, Valpolicella Ripasso, which is a label designation to remember, is made with partially dried grape skins (more on this in a moment) that have been left over from grapes used in the production of Amarone. A good Valpolicella can start well under $20 and climb up from there.

FAST FACT

Clinton is the name of an aromatic, low-production red wine made in Veneto that's essentially banned from distribution because it doesn't meet DOC rules. But if you find yourself in the area, keep an eye out, because some local spots still serve it.

Amarone

Amarone ("am-a-rhone-ee") is one of the top wines of Italy and, according to almost any wine critic, also one of the highest-quality wines in the world. It's made in the Valpolicella zone from the same varietals that are typically found in Valpolicella-labeled wines.

The main difference is that the grapes used in Amarone are harvested last, so they are as ripe as possible. In a method that's fairly unique to the region, the ultra-ripe grapes are then dried and pressed, resulting in wines that are highly concentrated, big and full-bodied.

You wouldn't want to pair your Amarone with a light salad. These wines exhibit strong plum, raisin (hence the dried grapes), deep fruit and chocolate flavors – perfect for hearty, red meat-dominated cuisine.

Amarone bottles can be found in the $30 range, but the lower-priced ones don't hold a candle to the similarly priced, or even lower-priced, standard Valpolicella wines. You pay a premium for the Amarone name, so if you're going to indulge, we recommend going a little further upstream and treating yourself to a very nice wine.

Bardolino

Bardolino ("bar-doe-lee-no") is located about 80 miles west of Venice, and the main grapes used to make these popular red wines are Corvina and Rondinella, along with smaller parts of less-recognized local varietals. Bardolino wines are much lighter and less complex than their Valpolicella and Amarone counterparts, making them a good choice when you're jonesing for a little red wine on a hot summer day.

They are best consumed young and pair well with antipasti, salads or chicken dishes. Bardolino wines classify as DOC status.

One of the Bardolino wines we bought when writing this seemed to be widely available – the 2013 Montresor Bardolino Le Banche, which was fresh and fruity. A nice buy for $14.

Bardolino Superiore is classified as DOCG, and the wines spend a little more time aging than the standard Bardolino. They come with a slightly higher price tag too.

Soave

Soave ("so-ah-vay") is the main white wine from the Veneto region that you'll find on wine lists and at your local wine shop. It's a great one to know about since it's usually priced reasonably (often under $15) and is an excellent, refreshing, crowd-pleasing white.

The likely reason it's not a runaway hit in the United States is simply because people don't know what it is. White wine drinkers tend to stick with varietals they know, and the main grape used in the production of Soave is Garganega — clearly not the grape you hear people conversing about at dinner parties.

The beauty of Soave wines, and their incredibly low price points, is a prime example of the importance of trying new regions and varietals. A few years ago, when Andrew was deep in his study of different varietals, he bought a 1.5-liter bottle of Soave for $14 at his wine retailer. He was buying a bulk white wine for a party and had heard Soave was a good bargain. Upon opening this bottle, he couldn't believe how pleasant the wine was. He immediately questioned spending $20 on a Sauvignon Blanc, because the big bottle of Soave proved to be much more enjoyable and a perfect summer wine.

Prosecco

Prosecco ("pro-seck-oh") wines are mildly bubbly, crisp whites produced in Veneto. It can be a more accessible bubbly than a Brut or champagne, with its fizz toned down, making it a popular aperitif that pairs well with a variety of cheeses and light fare. Prosecco wines have light floral aromas with flavors of pear, apple and citrus.

These wines are made from the Glera grape, an Italian white varietal that many people have consumed but aren't familiar with by name.

Prosecco wines are excellent values, starting in the $10 range and going up from there, making them less expensive than most of the California Bruts or French Champagnes you might enjoy under similar circumstances. In short, they're the perfect wine to bring to a dinner party or bust out for a celebratory occasion.

FAST FACT

The town of Verona, which is surrounded by many of the region's finest vineyards, is the setting for Shakespeare's *Romeo and Juliet*.

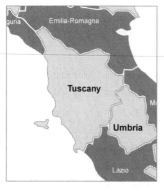

TUSCANY (TOSCANA)

The hits just keep coming as we move to the central part of Italy. Tuscany, which is probably the most universally recognized region of Italian wines, is also one of the oldest wine-producing regions in the world.

It appears, based on expert analysis of early cave drawings and pottery markings, that winemaking in Tuscany began as early as the 4th century B.C. when the area was first inhabited by the Etruscans. Back then, it's believed that Sangiovese grapes grew in the wild, and the Etruscans began creating wine with them.

Tuscany's picturesque landscape of rolling green hills is a perfect environment for grape growing. Many of the best-known vineyards are located high on the hills, which shield the grapes from extreme summer temperatures.

In Tuscany, Sangiovese is the primary grape varietal, but virtually every popular grape you can recite is also planted here. This includes red grapes such as Cabernet Sauvignon, Cabernet Franc, Merlot, Syrah and even Pinot Noir, along with other, less-common local red grapes. Among white grapes, Trebbiano is among the most prevalent, but you'll also find Chardonnay and Sauvignon Blanc.

When we think of Tuscan reds, there are four wines that are top of mind: Brunello, Chianti, Vino Nobile di Montepulciano and Super Tuscans. Let's take a brief look at each one.

Brunello

It's hard to find a bottle of Brunello ("brue-nell-oh") priced under $25 or $30, and there's a good reason why. Like Amarone, and the other Italian "B's" Barolo and Barbaresco, Brunello is a world-class wine.

Brunello wines are made 100 percent from Sangiovese that's grown near the town of Montalcino, and many Brunellos will make this clear with the designator "Brunello di Montalcino" on the label. Here, as in many regions of Italy, Sangiovese really flourishes, so much so that the locals just refer to Sangiovese as Brunello. You might too as you begin to taste them.

Brunello wines are well-structured, well-balanced, age-worthy reds. Because the character of the grapes can vary depending on the elevation where they're grown, Brunello wines can range in body from light to medium to full bodied, and the flavors can change as well. Some have a dusty red cherry flavor to them, while others can carry more oak notes.

These are highly tannic wines when they're young, and they're meant to be laid down for several years to give time for the tannins to chill out and soften.

Note: If, like us, you can't always wait for your wines to age, or are looking for good value, check out Rosso di Montalcino wines, which are not aged as long and are more approachable when they're young.

Chianti

Chianti ("key-ahn-tee") is a relatively common wine term for most early-stage wine consumers, and it's often thought of as "an Italian wine," or even an Italian wine varietal, rather than as a geographical location. But Chianti is the largest winemaking area in Tuscany, and its wines are labeled across two zones, Chianti and Chianti Classico.

Under the official rules, Chianti has to include at least 70 percent Sangiovese, so if you're drinking a Chianti, you're drinking (mostly) Sangiovese. Chianti can also include up to 10 percent Canaiolo, a standard Tuscan red blending grape, and up to 15 percent of other red grape varietals, such as Cabernet Sauvignon and Merlot. So as you can imagine, when you look across the spread of different winemakers in the region, not one bottle of Chianti is likely to have the same varietal composition. That's just one more reason why drinking Chianti wines is so much fun (and a long journey).

And if you're looking for more fun, you can jump in and begin tasting wines from Chianti Classico. Contrary to many people's beliefs, Chianti Classico isn't just "Classic Chianti." It's a specific geographic area right in the heart of Chianti. The land, soil, elevation and winemaking methods are slightly different, and according to many aficionados, perhaps better than those in Chianti.

One key difference is that Chianti Classico rules dictate that 80 percent of the wine must be made from Sangiovese, compared to 70 percent for Chianti. The only way to find out what you prefer is to give all these different areas and subregions a try.

Vino Nobile di Montepulciano

Vino Nobile di Montepulciano ("vee-no no-bee-lay dee mon-tee-pul-chee-ah-no") rounds out the trifecta of fantastic wines originating from this region (excluding Super Tuscans), yet Chianti and Brunello remain the most well-known across much of the world. As a result, Vino Nobile di Montepulciano can be scored for half the price (or less) of Brunellos while still being loaded with the awesome flavor representative of the terroir.

Vino Nobile di Montepulciano is defined as the wine that comes from the vineyards surrounding Montepulciano, a city in the southeastern part of Tuscany. It was one of the first wines to achieve DOC status, and later grabbed the DOCG badge with guidelines that stated the wine must be based on a minimum of 70 percent of Sangiovese along with 30 percent of other grapes (frequently Canaiolo Nero, although many producers seem to prefer more and more Sangiovese-dominated blends). Vino Nobile di Montepulciano wines must also be aged for a minimum of 24 months (36 months for Riserva).

These wines exhibit aromas of dark cherry and plum with a touch of pepper, and flavors of red fruit (strawberry, cherry). Depending on the producer's style, the wines of Vino Nobile di Montepulciano can offer the bold richness of Brunellos, with similar grape varietal composition, at a fraction of the price. They are typically a little less dusty and dry then their grape expressions in nearby Chianti.

As its regal-sounding name suggests, Vino Nobile di Montepulciano is a wine you need to experience. Dig in and enjoy.

Super Tuscans

It's always fun to write about "rogue movements," but there aren't a whole lot to choose from in the annals of wine history. But back in the 1970s, as Chianti sales slumped, a group of maverick winemakers went out on a limb and experimented outside the rules. And today we can all reap the benefits, as the "Super Tuscans" wine rebellion allows us to enjoy amazing wines at fantastic prices.

So what did the producers of Super Tuscans do that was so special? Well, they simply threw out the rulebook that dictated what percentage of varietals each wine had to have. And with almost every major grape varietal grown in Tuscany, they had a lot to work with.

As a result, Super Tuscan wines will run the gamut. Some are produced with lots of Sangiovese or just a small percentage of Sangiovese. Others are produced with more Merlot and Cabernet Sauvignon. And still others will use Syrah, Cabernet Franc, or a proprietary blend of any of these grapes. This freedom enables talented winemakers to create new styles and expressions of their wines.

In the opening pages of this book we referenced the Antinori Solaia, a Super Tuscan that could sit alongside the finest Bordeaux. Tenuta San Guido's Sassicaia is another well-known Super Tuscan, widely available for a little more than $100 (depending on the year), and a world-class offering in that price range.

On the opposite end of the spectrum are wines such as the Frescobaldi Remole Toscana Rosso, a good wine that can be scored for as little as $12.

When you visit your local wine shop, you won't see the words "Super Tuscan" written on the label. So, look for Tuscan wines with the IGT classification, many of which will simply be labeled as "Rosso" or "Toscana Rosso." (For more on decoding Super Tuscan wine labels, see Chapter 9.) Experiment and see what you like!

FAST FACT

In the classic oenophile favorite *Sideways*, Miles (Paul Giamatti) asks Maya (Virginia Madsen) what bottle made her serious about drinking wine. Her response? A 1988 Sassicaia. Not coincidentally, *Sideways* director Alexander Payne has cited this Super Tuscan as one of his all-time favorite wines.

Carmignano

As we discuss Super Tuscans, we'd be remiss not to mention Carmignano ("car-min-yah-no"). This area of Tuscany was blending wines outside the standard classification system long before the rise of the Super Tuscans. Because of Carmignano's long history of growing and using Cabernet Sauvignon and Cabernet Franc grapes, this region was in effect grandfathered in to allow blends with a higher percentage of these varietals. To those in the know, Carmignano is often considered the birthplace of the "Super Tuscan."

UMBRIA

Located almost in the dead center of the country, Umbria is the only Italian region that doesn't touch either the sea or another country. The lush "green heart of Italy" is home to a few semi-famous towns, including regional capital Perugia and scenic Assisi. More importantly, its gorgeous countryside yields not only excellent wines but also a bounty of olives that are used for another famous Italian export: olive oil.

Though not a huge wine producer in terms of volume — it ranks near the bottom quartile in this area — Umbria produces several key wines worth your attention. The region is best known for its whites, led by the crisp Orvieto, with about 60 percent of Umbria's overall production focused on white wines. But there are some notable DOCG reds to keep an eye out for as well, at least one of which you stand a decent chance of finding in North America. Let's dig in.

Orvieto

Umbria's most famous wine town is legendary for its wine of the same name. One of Italy's best-selling DOC whites, Orvieto ("or-vee-yet-oh") uses the Trebbiano grape as its base, with 40 percent to 60 percent of the wine consisting of Trebbiano. Today these wines typically boast a golden pale color and deliver a soft, crisp taste, making Orvieto a nice wine to sip on a hot summer day or pair with some antipasti. At a typical price point in the $10 to $15 range, and sometimes even below $10, this is a fun white to mix into your collection without breaking the bank.

Sagrantino di Montefalco

In the modest hill town of Montefalco lies a little gem of a grape, native to the area, called the Sagrantino ("sah-gran-tee-no"). Though this DOCG wine can be tough to find, for many aficionados its unique nature and big, bold drinking characteristics make it worth the time – and the price tag, which usually runs in the $30s or $40s.

The striking scarlet color pairs with an aromatic nose that combines spices (nutmeg, cinnamon) and fruits (raspberry, blueberry and cherry) to beguiling effect. Drinking is an intense experience, with a lot of thickness and tannins that are ideally softened over time.

This is a wine that will reward aging and makes an excellent accompaniment for hearty fare such as red meats, spicy pastas and rich cheeses.

ABRUZZO

Located in the central east part of Italy, with the "administrative center" of L'Aquila about 120 kilometers northeast of Rome, Abruzzo has some unique geographical characteristics that make it particularly conducive to producing wines. Situated between the Adriatic Sea to the east and the Apennines and Maiella mountain ranges to the west, this is some beautiful country: Abruzzo has the most national parks and forests of any Italian region.

Two-thirds of the countryside is mountainous, and when you combine the region's low hills with the dry breezes coming off the Adriatic, it can make for some pretty stellar grape-growing conditions.

The result is a region that's the fifth most voluminous wine-producing region in Italy. Only about 20 percent of that output falls under the DOC or DOCG classifications, but among that percentage you'll find some pretty strong wines.

Montepulciano d'Abruzzo

Not to be confused with Vino Nobile di Montepulciano, a tasty Tuscan wine made primarily from Sangiovese, these wines are made from the Montepulciano ("mohn-tay-pul-chee-ah-no) grape. Though not a household name, Montepulciano is the fifth most widely planted red grape variety in Italy.

Generally these wines must consist of at least 85 percent Montepulciano, with Sangiovese typically permitted up to 15 percent. (A few areas require 100 percent Montepulciano.)

These are some of the best values around, with delicious wines to be had in the $10 to $15 range (and sometimes even cheaper!) and up from there. Deep red and full-bodied but smooth, these are highly drinkable, versatile wines that typically contain hints of pepper and spice. Great with food or served straight up, you simply must make these a regular part of your wine rotation.

Trebbiano d'Abruzzo

As the name suggests, the Trebbiano grape is the foundation for the light, dry DOC wines of the Abruzzo region. Though on the acidic side, they typically yield a more subtle drinking experience with light floral characteristics that make this a solid white alternative to the basic Chardonnays or Pinot Grigios you've probably drank a couple hundred times. At a price point around $10, and sometimes less, why not give one a try next time you're looking for a bottle to take to the pool or bring with you on a picnic?

CAMPANIA

Naples. The Amalfi Coast. Mt. Vesuvius. And the birthplace of an obscure food called pizza. Yep, Campania has a lot of culture and history going for it — including wine. But its greatness isn't just in the past — even if the ancient Greeks did introduce several key varietals to the area. Rather, with a variety of delicious whites and hearty reds unique to the area — and whose grapes thrive in the volcanic soil surrounding Vesuvius — Campania is helping lead the rise of Southern Italian wines.

We think you'll find a growing selection of wines from Campania at wine stores and on restaurant lists in the years to come, but for now the pickings are still fairly slim. Here are some choice ones to keep an eye out for:

Falanghina

This captivating white, based on the grape of the same name, has an intense fruity taste – hints of peach, pear, grapefruit and orange can often be found in these wines – with a smooth, more moderate finish. Mmm.

Typically priced around $15, Falanghina ("fah-lahn-ghee-nah") makes an excellent accompaniment for fish or white meat, but can just as easily be enjoyed on its own. One of Campania's primary white grapes, we expect to see more of it in the upcoming years and highly recommend you add it to your wine-drinking arsenal.

Coda di Volpe

This one is a little tougher to find than the other two whites listed here, but worth the effort for those who enjoy fuller-bodied whites, such as chardonnay, but are looking for something a little more exotic. The name translates to "tail of the fox," a moniker given for the bushy shape of the grape bunches.

Coda di Volpe ("co-dah dee vohl-pay") is golden yellow in color, aromatic on the nose and offers an interesting mix of sweetness and spice. You get some citrusy fruits mingling with light notes of nuttiness. You'll find Coda di Volpe both in single-varietal wines and blended with the other regional whites listed here (among others).

Greco di Tufo

If you think white wines lack personality, check this one out. This DOCG wine is one of Southern Italy's finest whites, and legend has it that it dates back to around 750 B.C., when Greek colonists introduced it to Campania ("Greco" is the Italian word for "Greek").

Whatever the case, this wine is a tasty treat, full-bodied and well-balanced with shades of pear, citrus and honey mingling with some mineraly goodness and just the right amount of acidity. It's made of at least 85 percent Greco with the remainder consisting of Coda di Volpe. Serve it up with your favorite grilled fish or seafood risotto, or enjoy it solo with some good company.

Aglianico

This varietal, covered in greater detail in Chapter 4, is the predominant red in Campania. You'll find it most often selling under its own name at around $15 a pop, and it's a delicious accompaniment for some of the hearty dishes that come out of Southern Italy.

Also, keep an eye out for Taurasi, a mouthwatering DOCG wine made of at least 85 percent Aglianico. It typically runs closer to $40 and has been called "the Barolo of the South." Taurasi can be tough to find but is worth the splurge if you come across a bottle.

SICILY

Sicily is an island rich in history, culture and cuisine, even known by some as "God's Kitchen." And inside God's Kitchen, you'll find some fantastic wine that's quickly working its way onto the global stage.

You might not have guessed that if your first thought of Sicily was a group of burly mafia men carrying out shady backroom dealings.

Part of the reason for the large number of vineyards is that the area is known for dessert wines that require a high concentration of grapes, the most famous of which is Marsala.

Marsala is another example of the close correlation between wine and cuisine in Italian culture. For many, "Chicken Marsala" is the first association that comes to mind when they hear the word "Marsala."

Nero d'Avola

Nero d'Avola is the big red wine made in Sicily, and it's rapidly growing in popularity, leading us to believe it could be the next Malbec in terms of commanding its own shelf space in wine shops.

Nero d'Avola is a black grape that produces wines that are very dark in color with strong herbal aromas and pepper and spice.

These wines are excellent to pair with food and are markedly different in character than many of the other Italian wines covered here. We find them to offer a lot of complexity for the money. Many excellent Nero d'Avola bottles can be found in the $10 to $20 range, a fantastic value compared to similarly priced wines produced elsewhere in the world.

Lots of wine consumers walk past bottles of Nero d'Avola every trip to the store and don't think about experimenting with a wine they aren't familiar with or a grape varietal that isn't a household name in the United States. For this reason, we're big proponents of trying something new as often as possible when you visit your local wine store.

Believe it or not, a random purchase of a $12 Nero d'Avola a few years ago first turned Andrew on to the grape. And he's continued to pair it with meals ever since.

FAST FACT

Sicily has more vineyards than any other region in Italy, yet Sicilians consume less wine per capita than any other region in Italy.

CHAPTER 7:
ITALIAN WINE VINTAGE REPORT

Sooner or later, it's going to happen. You find a bottle of wine you adore. You file it in your mental Rolodex for future reference, and then a few months or a year down the line, you see that same bottle sitting on the shelf. You go home and crack it open in expectation of pure deliciousness, but the magic is missing. What the @#$%&! is going on?

In many cases, the culprit is that little four-digit vintage number on the label, which can be easy to overlook in your excitement about finding a certain bottle. And it's why, to get a full picture of the Italian wine you're drinking (or considering drinking), you'll need to understand the importance of the vintage number, or year the grapes were harvested, you'll find on every wine label.

One of the great aspects to enjoying and experiencing wine is that it changes every year. Because the growing of grapes is really an agricultural activity, its success is heavily dictated by the weather. And we all know how unpredictable weather can be.

CHAPTER 7: ITALIAN WINE VINTAGE REPORT

With grapes such as Nebbiolo, which is known as a difficult grape to grow, winemakers have to contend with factors outside their control every season. You'll notice that certain vintages will be priced higher than others as you peruse your local wine shop, and much of this variance depends on the growing conditions that year and the correlating grape quality.

At restaurants it can be even trickier since some wine lists won't include the vintage (don't hesitate to ask), while others may only list one choice of vintage on a particular wine. If you're selecting a higher-end wine, it never hurts to ask the sommelier if they have a bottle from a different year, as sometimes your better buy might be a lesser bottle from a great year instead of a well-regarded producer in a challenging year.

Fortunately for wine fans, we're in the midst of an incredible run of strong vintages of Italian wine. With the exception of 2002, anything from 2000 to today has been a banner year for Italian grape growing. 2007 in Piedmont and Tuscany is known as one of the better years on record from the past several decades.

You probably won't see many 2002 bottles still lingering around your wine shop, so you're pretty safe choosing any vintage across most of the regions of Italy. But pay attention to future vintages. In California's Napa region, for instance, 2011 was a particularly nasty year for grape growing, with flooding limiting much of the crop.

In the case of a bad growing year, the best producers will release smaller quantities of their best grapes. But other producers may try to squeeze out as much as they can, not thrilled about having to take a big financial hit.

Wine Spectator magazine and *Wine Advocate* critic Robert Parker frequently post vintage charts indicating how they felt the growing year panned out. They travel to almost every wine region and meet with producers, so their insight is invaluable. *Wine Spectator* even has a free mobile app with a vintage chart by region that we find helpful. Of course, you can always ask your local wine shop owner for their thoughts.

As you progress in your wine journey, recognizing vintages will become second nature. You'll soon gravitate toward those years you know to be better (or the ones you prefer), and you'll be able to compare prices accordingly. We always keep an eye out for good buys on the best vintages. Once these wines are gone, they can never come back.

CHAPTER 8:
AGING OF ITALIAN WINES:
UNLOCKING THE HIDDEN POTENTIAL OF WELL-STRUCTURED WINES

Many high-end Italian wines are built for the long haul. That young bottle of Brunello you cracked open last week, for example, might taste completely different in seven to 10 years. And if you're dropping some serious coin on a bottle, you want to make sure that "different" means complex and mouth-watering rather than sour and vinegary. So how can you find that sweet spot at which the wine is best for consumption?

We tend to believe that identifying the point in a wine's age at which it's most enjoyable is really an individual thing. You'll find several references throughout this book to aging different Italian wines, but there's no one right answer for any of them.

You have to experiment a bit. One of our favorite tricks is to buy three bottles of a wine you enjoy. Drink one right away. Save one for another occasion down the line. And hold on to the third for as long as you desire based on how that second one tasted to you.

Some people don't like older wines. When you pop the cork, you can get a dusty hardcover book aroma that turns some people away. After a few hours in a decanter, though, you might be surprised how much older wines can open up, and how they can change over the course of time.

This is very much the fun of buying high-quality Italian wines. It's almost a game to find the longevity cycle you prefer the most. And the game remains ever-challenging since new vintages are always being introduced — some better than others, and all with unique characteristics you'll have to experience to understand.

We don't want this to sound overwhelming. While aging Italian wines isn't an exact science, there are some guidelines that can help you as you begin experimenting.

REDS ARE MORE FREQUENTLY BUILT FOR THE LONG HAUL ...

The first thing to consider is that red wines are built differently, with stronger tannins and structure that allow the wines to evolve over time, absorb the tannins and create soft, fluffy, highly flavorful wines that are an absolute joy to drink.

White wines, save certain dessert wines, are built to be consumed young, and time in the cellar won't do as much to make them better.

We aren't saying they'll spoil in just a handful of years, but if you're going to hold on to something for 10 years, you'll be much better served with an age-worthy red wine.

... BUT NOT ALL REDS ARE GOOD CANDIDATES FOR AGING

Many reds with lighter tannins and acidity are ready to drink now. Most of the sub-$20 bottles of Chianti you'll come across, for example, aren't the best candidates for long-term aging. Many of them can go for a while, but they'll hit their plateau sooner than a big Barolo or Brunello.

This isn't to say that all expensive bottles are meant to be aged either. Some normally strong wines from bad growing years might not be ones you want to spend the money on to age for a decade.

The quality and structure of the wine and the vintage are the best attributes to look at when deciding what to age. Find a hefty, big-in-the-mouth, tannic and tight Barolo from a good year that just kicks you in the face. That's the one you might want to age for a while.

MANY ITALIAN WINES HAVE ALREADY BEEN AGED FOR YOU

Remember those Riserva wines we covered? Many Brunellos and Barolos will be aged in barrels for a few years, and then spend a few more in the bottle before they're even released to the public. Much of this is governed under Italian winemaking rules and representative of a region's unique regulations.

This isn't to say that these wines are done and ready to drink. Some of them may be. Others are still in their infancy.

The Antinori Solaia we opened this book with was very young when Andrew consumed it. It had a decade to run, maybe more. On the other hand, we recently enjoyed some 10-year-old Brunellos that tasted like they were bottled yesterday. We wish we had given them another five to 10 years.

It's a game, and a challenging one at that. Here are some quick thoughts on some of the most popular, cellarable Italian wines and suggestions for how long they can go:

- **Barbaresco:** good ones can go for 10-14 years, maybe longer
- **Barolo:** 10-12 years, with top Barolos going for 20-25 years

- **Amarone:** can go almost forever, 20+ years with a good vintage
- **Brunello:** another heavy hitter; good vintages can go 20-30 years, peaking right around then
- **Super Tuscans:** this one is a moving target given the variety of wine styles, but the good ones can go for several decades

MOST BOTTLES AT YOUR WINE SHOP AREN'T INTENDED FOR LONG AGING

We'd venture to guess that 80 percent to 90 percent of the bottles you encounter at your average wine shop aren't meant to age beyond the five-to seven-year time frame. The reason? Higher-end wines just don't move as fast as your typical $12 Super Tuscan, so shops will likely carry only a few meant to go the distance.

That's OK, because unless you're flush with cash, this means you don't have to worry about aging more than 80 percent of the wines you buy.

In other words, just kick back and don't agonize over whether you should age your garden-variety Chianti for 10 years — it's not going to deliver more than it would have seven years prior.

But when you find that nicely structured, highly tannic Amarone that you enjoyed when it was young, take that second bottle and hold it: You may have a completely new appreciation for the wine when you taste it after 10 to 15 years.

In the wine world, this is one more fun game to play. It can get expensive, but there's nothing like opening a 15-year-old Brunello you've been holding on to and enjoying it with special friends and family.

And one final suggestion: Store wines in a cool dark environment with a consistent temperature. There's a huge business around creating the ideal conditions for aging, and you can go as far into it as you want. Often we've had great luck with a wine fridge or EuroCave, designed to hold a good temperature with little vibration and without sucking all the humidity up, which standard refrigerators tend to do.

Bottom line? Have fun with this one. After a few years, we're guessing you'll be pulling out 10-year Barolos to compare to your friend's 15-year-old Amarone. Crack them both and see how they've matured. We bet they still have some time to run.

CHAPTER 9:
READING AN ITALIAN WINE LABEL

T he world of Italian wine is deep and complex, and it's a little intimidating to dive all in and experiment with different wines, particularly when the label markings seem to be in a different language (and sometimes they are).

Why bet on a bottle with a funny name created in some unpronounceable region in Italy when you can buy a trusty Sonoma Chardonnay or Napa Merlot for the same price? The answer is simple: When you experiment with different wines, you build a larger base of knowledge from which to draw every time you choose a bottle. A second, but no less important, reason is that these wines are frequently delicious.

Plus, the time you spend experimenting serves as a virtual trip around the globe. You can learn a lot about the culture, winemaking practices and geography of the countries your wine originates in just from reading the label — without the jet lag, souvenir clutter and gnarly exchange rates that come with taking multiple trips abroad (not that there's anything wrong with that).

Decoding an Italian wine label isn't particularly difficult once you've educated yourself on the Italian wine classification system, developed an understanding of the main grape varietals, familiarized yourself with which grapes grow in which regions, and begun to recognize certain producers, vintages and brands. Whew.

OK, so maybe it isn't an overnight process. But it's not as challenging as navigating the *calle* of Venice either.

Look at it this way: Each part of an Italian wine label provides clues that, when put together, will often tell you more about that bottle than the simpler labels we're accustomed to seeing on U.S.-produced wines.

THE BASICS

Deciphering an Italian wine label bottle can be overwhelming because of the sheer mass of information provided — in a foreign language, no less. Here are six key clues to look for on an Italian wine label to help you pick the bottle you want:

1) **Wine name:** Seems straightforward, right? But location on the label can vary, and sometimes the "name" is also the estate or vineyard name, which can get confusing.

2) **Wine appellation, region and/or grape varietal:** Again, these won't always be spelled out for you. You'll have to use what you know about Italian geography and varietals to put the pieces of the puzzle together.

3) **Producer:** Often an intimidating, unpronounceable word or words.

4) **Classification (DOC, DOCG, IGT, Vino da tavola):** Must appear by law, unless you're sipping a glass in a small winery in the hills of Italy (good) or drinking a bottle your cousin "cultivated" from a homemade kit (likely bad).

5) Other classifying terms: Words like Classico, Superiore and Riserva (see Chapter 5) that can designate additional aging and production nuances.

6) Vintage: The year the wine was produced. Finally, something easy.

ADDITIONAL TERMINOLOGY

Though less common, you'll also come across these basic Italian words that describe the bottle's contents:

Bianco: white
Rosso: red
Dolce: sweet
Secco: dry
Spumante: sparkling

In addition to the above, some Italian wines will include even more detail about the vineyard and the land from which the wine was made – and we're not talking about the hilariously flowery language sometimes used to describe the winery's rolling hills and scenic vistas.

Here's a list of terms you may see, some more common than others, and their meaning:

Azienda Agricola: a farm that grows its own grapes, and may grow many other fruits and vegetables as well
Fattoria: a medium to large wine-growing property
Podere/Poderi: a small wine farm or property, sometimes part of a fattoria
Tenuta: a large estate
Vigna/Vigneto: a single vineyard that has a particular name (this is always a good sign)

LET THE DECODING BEGIN: 8 SAMPLE WINE LABELS TO PERUSE

Now let's take a look at eight different Italian wine labels, loosely organized from *facile* (easy) to *difficile* (difficult), to see how our newfound knowledge plays out:

1. **Grape/Region:** Chianti Classico (Sangiovese) from Tuscany

2. **Classification:** DOCG

3. **"Riserva"** — this wine has been aged longer by the producer

4. **Producer:** Banfi

Additional Notes: The vintage isn't listed here, but would likely be called out elsewhere on the bottle.

1. **Producer:** Colimoro
2. **Vintage:** 2010
3. **Grape/Region:** Montepulciano from Abruzzo
4. **Classification:** DOC
5. **"Six Months Oak Aged"** — Some similar wines are aged more, others less

---

1. **Grape/Region:** Dolcetto (light, easy-drinking red wine) from Asti (Piedmont region)
2. **Classification:** DOC
3. **Producer:** Casata Monticello
4. **Vintage:** 2007

1. **Vintage:** 2012
2. **Grape/Region:** Arneis (white grape) from Roero (wine district in Piedmont region)
3. **Classification:** DOCG
4. **Producer:** Giacomo Fenocchio

---

1. **"CastelGiocondo"** — the name of the wine, and also of the village/estate from where it hails
2. **"Riserva"** — this wine has been aged longer by the producer
3. **Vintage:** 2006
4. **Grape/Region:** Brunello (Sangiovese) from Montalcino (Tuscany)
5. **Classification:** DOCG
6. **Producer:** Marchesi de' Frescobaldi, one of the largest names in Italian wine

1. **Producer:** Pieropan

2. **Grape/Region:** Amarone (Corvina grape primarily, may be blended with others); region unspecified but most likely Valpolicella from Veneto

3. **"Vigna Garzon"** — indicates this is a single-vineyard wine

Additional Notes: The classification isn't listed here, but by law would appear elsewhere on the bottle. The vintage also isn't revealed on the front label, but again would likely be called out elsewhere on the bottle.

1. **Producer:** Bricco Asili

2. **Grape/Region:** Barbaresco (Nebbiolo grape) from Piedmont

3. **Classification:** DOCG

4. **"Bricco Asili"** (second time) — Also the name of the vineyard

5. **"Estate bottled"** — Indicates 100% of the grapes in the wine came from the winery listed on the label, and the wine was produced and bottled in the same area stated on the bottle

6. **"Azienda Agricola Ceretto"** – "Azienda Agricola" indicates a farming business, in this case one owned by the Ceretto group

Additional Notes: The vintage isn't listed here, but would likely be called out elsewhere on the bottle.

1. **"Crognolo"** — the name of the wine

2. **Vintage:** 2007 (this is a good sign – see Chapter 7)

3. **Grape/Region:** Grape unclear but possibly a blend of Sangiovese, Merlot and Cabernet (see section below); Tuscany

4. **Classification:** IGT

5. **Producer:** Tenuta Sette Ponti

6 QUICK TIPS FOR DECODING A SUPER TUSCAN WINE LABEL

Decoding Tuscan wines can present challenges for even veteran Italian wine drinkers since they fall outside regional norms – and their labels reflect that.

But as we mention in the "Regions" chapter, Super Tuscans represent some of the best Italian wines out there, so you don't want to miss out just because the label renders the contents a mystery. Here are six quick tips to help you identify and decode a Super Tuscan:

1) **Find the region.** Are the words "Toscana" or "Tuscany" on the bottle? Congratulations, you've found yourself a wine made in Tuscany. But don't get too cocky yet.

2) **Look for key words and phrases indicating wine types.** Chianti, Brunello or Vino Nobile di Montepulciano? These are all made in Tuscany, but they adhere to the rules of the region, so they're not part of the rogue movement known as Super Tuscans. On a positive note, they're typically quite tasty.

3) **Locate the classification.** With rare exception, Super Tuscans will fall into the IGT category.

4) **Think three grapes.** Super Tuscan wine labels often won't indicate the grapes used within. But many are made with some blend of Sangiovese, Merlot and Cabernet, so use that as a baseline and work from there.

5) **Turn the bottle over.** In some cases the back of a wine label will yield nothing more than undecipherable markings or generic promotional copy, but in other instances it can provide important information regarding a wine's composition and the producer's growing practices.

6) **Search that smartphone.** Still at a loss? In many cases, a Google search can yield specific grape percentages, customer reviews and other info that can help you determine whether to buy that bottle.

EPILOGUE: DON'T JUDGE A BOTTLE BY ITS LABEL

Each person's wine journey is individual to them, a personal experience that you shape. Knowing what you like and why you like it is the name of the game, because then you'll be able to visit the wine shop, search for bottles with similar details, and begin to differentiate styles and traits between the wine producers.

This granular study is where wine tasting gets really interesting. Grapes from two estates adjacent to each other can be grown in similar climates and weather conditions, in virtually identical soil, but the winemaking practices of the estates can shape the wines' personality, making them quite different when they hit the bottle.

Remember to keep your mind open, try everything and follow what you like — which may not always be what others tell you that you should like.

CHAPTER 10:
READING AN ITALIAN RESTAURANT WINE LIST

S ince you don't have the luxury of browsing at your leisure, decoding a restaurant wine list can often be more stressful than strolling the aisles of a wine shop, especially if an overtasked *cameriere* is breathing down your neck awaiting your order.

If you're like us, at some point you've gone out to eat and found yourself staring blankly at the wine list, your mind racing to make sense of the indecipherable text while beads of perspiration start forming on your forehead. Wait, I'm paying for this?

Next time you dine out, we want your biggest challenge to be deciding whether to order a can't-miss Chianti, sample a Nero d'Avola you've never seen, or splurge on a bottle of Amarone.

To help expand your comfort zone, let's take a look at a sample wine list from Sotto Sotto, one of Atlanta's best Italian restaurants, and break down a few entries.

1 ➤

Piemonte	Glass	Bottle
117 Gavi 'La Rocca', Coppo 2010	$9.00	$36.00
147 Chardonnay 'Costeblanche', Coppo 2009	$10.00	$40.00
110 Chardonnay 'L'Altro', Pio Cesare 2009		$45.00
106 Roero Arneis, Vietti 2011	$12.00	$48.00

1) Gavi 'La Rocca', Coppo 2010

Gavi: The type of wine, in this case made from the Cortese grape

La Rocca: The estate where the wine was produced

Coppo: The winemaker

2010: The vintage

2 ➤

Friuli-Venezia Giulia	Glass	Bottle
105 Pinot Grigio Venezia Giulia, Jermann 2009	$12.00	$48.00
137 Pinot Bianco Collio, Schiopetto 2008		$60.00
115 Sauvignon Blanc Friuli Grave, Villa Chiòpris 2010	$9.00	$36.00
129 Sauvignon Blanc Collio, Russiz Superiore 2009		$48.00
142 Chardonnay/Sauvignon/Picolit Venezia Giulia 'Vespa', Bastianich 2008		$70.00
143 Friulano Colli Orientali del Friuli 'Plus', Bastianich 2007		$115.00

2) Pinot Grigio Venezia Giulia, Jermann 2009

Pinot Grigio: The grape / type of wine

Venezia Giulia: The region in which it was produced

Jermann: The winemaker

2009: The vintage

3 ➤

Veneto	Glass	Bottle
241 Valpolicella Classico Superiore, Monte del Frá 2008	$11.00	$44.00
227 Valpolicella Superiore 'Ripassa', Zenato 2008		$58.00
275 Valpolicella Classico Superiore, Giuseppe Quintarelli 2000		$130.00
271 Valpolicella/Amarone 'Pario', L'Arco 2004		$70.00
228 Amarone della Valpolicella Classico, Tommasi 2007		$115.00
230 Amarone della Valpolicella Classico, Zenato 2007		$135.00
299 Amarone della Valpolicella Classico 'Corte Brà', Sartori 2006		$85.00

3) Valpolicella Classico Superiore, Monte del Frá 2008

Valpolicella: The type of wine, in this case a blend of Corvina
and Rondinella

Classico Superiore: Quality classification indicating premium
status, higher alcohol content and longer aging

Monte del Frá: The winemaker

2008: The vintage

Sicilia	Glass	Bottle
274 Nero d'Avola 'Lamùri', Tasca d'Almerita 2009	$10.00	$40.00

4) Nero d'Avola 'Lamùri', Tasca d'Almerita 2009

Nero d'Avola: The grape / type of wine

Lamùri: The name of the wine, roughly translating to "reasons of the heart" or "love' in Sicilian dialect

Tasca d'Almerita: The winemaker

2009: The vintage

Le Marche	Glass	Bottle
140 Verdicchio di Castelli di Jesi, 'Fontevecchia', Casalfarnato 2010	$9.00	$36.00
144 Verdicchio di Matelica, La Monacesca 2009		$55.00

5) Verdicchio di Castelli di Jesi, 'Fontevecchia', Casalfarneto 2010

Verdicchio: The grape / type of wine

Castelli di Jesi: The specific region where the wine is produced

Fontevecchia: The name of the wine

Casalfarneto: The winemaker

Piemonte	Glass	Bottle
222 Nebbiolo/Barbera Monferrato 'Pin', La Spinetta 2008		$100.00
287 Nebbiolo d'Alba 'Ochetti, Renato Ratti 2009	$12.00	$48.00
205 Gattinara, Giancarlo Travaglini 2006		$70.00
283 Barbaresco, Prunotto 2008		$100.00
214 Barbaresco, Piazzo 2006 (375 ml)		$44.00
321 Barbaresco 'Camp Gros Martinenga', Marchesi di Gresy 2005		$160.00

6) Nebbiolo/Barbera Monferrato 'Pin', La Spinetta 2008

Nebbiolo/Barbera: The blend of grapes, in this case 65 percent Nebbiolo and 35 percent Barbera

Monferrato: The specific region where the wine was produced, in this case in the Southeast corner of Piedmont

Pin: The name of the wine

La Spinetta: The winemaker

2008: The vintage

7 —249 | Umbria | Bottle
| Sagrantino di Montefalco 'Pagliaro', Paolo Bea 2005 | $165.00

7) Sagrantino di Montefalco 'Pagliaro,' Paolo Bea 2005

Sagrantino: The grape / type of wine

Montefalco: The specific area where this wine was produced, in this case a town in the central part of Umbria

Pagliaro: The name of the wine

Paolo Bea: The winemaker

2005: The vintage

Note: In this example, the wine list is conveniently organized by region. But in most instances, this won't be the case. Often, the restaurant will list the region at the end of an entry. Failing that, you'll have to use the knowledge you've gained here to ferret out the selection's geographical origins.

CHAPTER 11:
ITALIAN FOOD AND WINE

"A tavola non si invecchia."
("You don't age while seated for a meal.")

"Esse nufesso qui dice male di macaroni."
("One has to be an idiot to speak badly of macaroni.")

If you have an interest in Italian wine, chances are pretty good you also have a love for Italian food. The two are a match made in culinary heaven. And that's no coincidence.

Historically, Italians rarely dined without wine, and a region's wine was crafted to be "food-friendly," often with bright acidity that's a perfect match for cuisine. While some Italian wines may seem tannic, lean or tart by themselves, they'll often show a different profile when paired with boldly flavored Italian foods. It's a deliciously symbiotic relationship: food tastes better with wine, and vice-versa.

Today, as in most of the world, Italian families are more fragmented and lifestyles are more hectic, so it's not as much of a given that wine will be drank on a daily basis during meals. But it's still an essential part of the Italian dining experience, contributing to the spirited conversation, camaraderie and bonding that's typical of mealtime in Italy.

Fortunately, for those who live outside Italy, we live in a time when we can benefit from centuries spent perfecting wine and food — and the marriage of the two. And we can do it with incredible ease. We can simply walk into any grocery store, find plenty of fresh ingredients to create an authentic Italian meal based on a plethora of online recipes, and buy a bottle of wine made from grapes produced halfway across the world.

In the media, pasta and pizza are the dominant images when it comes to Italian food. And while you can find plenty of each throughout Italy, the country's cuisine is a lot more complex than that. Each region, city and town often has its own culinary traditions and specialties, each scrumptious in its own right, with locals often pairing these dishes with wines from the region. (For more on Italian food and wine pairings, see Appendix I.)

Traditionally, lunch was the big meal in Italy, with families returning home for generous feasts that typically consisted of a "primo piatto" (pasta or risotto) and secondo piatto (meat and vegetable), with appetizer, cheese and/or dessert courses often in the mix. Again, with today's busier lifestyles, this is no longer a given — some Italians eat shorter lunches, some have bigger dinners, and others only have a full-on family feast on Sundays.

FAST FACT

As of 2012, there were about 450 McDonald's restaurants operating in Italy (1 for every 136,000 Italians), compared to more than 14,000 in the United States (1 for every 23,000 Americans).

Regardless, it's no coincidence that the "Slow Food" movement was born in Italy. The concept of enjoying a meal based on fresh, locally produced ingredients at a leisurely pace endures. At restaurants, patrons often have to track down the waiter for the check, unlike in many cases here in North America, where it can feel like you're being hustled out the door. And the enjoyment of wine as a way to enhance a lengthy meal with family and friends remains an important part of this dining experience. *Buon appetito!*

CHAPTER 12:
THE SWEET LIFE:
ITALIAN WINE AND MOVIES

O utside of sipping a nice glass of Italian wine with a heaping bowl of pasta, one of the best ways to enjoy a bottle of vino is to pair it with an Italian film.

Italian cinema has a history that's nearly as rich as that of its wine, having given the world internationally renowned movie stars (Sophia Loren, Marcello Mastroianni), directors (Federico Fellini, Sergio Leone) and films (*Cinema Paradiso*, *Life Is Beautiful*).

In addition, Italian-American directors such as Martin Scorsese (*Goodfellas*, *Raging Bull*) and Francis Ford Coppola (the *Godfather* trilogy, *Apocalypse Now*) have helmed some of the best films of the last 50 years (and in the latter's case, embarked on a successful second career as a wine producer).

Yet for all the classic Italian films that have graced the silver screen, few have incorporated wine as a significant story element. Perhaps the reason is that since wine is such an integral part of Italian culture, there's no reason to bring further attention to it.

CHAPTER 12: THE SWEET LIFE: ITALIAN WINE AND MOVIES

That said, there are a few notable occasions in which Italian film and wine have intersected in memorable fashion. Here are 10 Italian movies that feature wine in some capacity and make a great match for cracking a bottle.

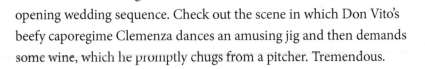

1) *The Godfather* **(1972):** Coppola's mafia epic about the fictional Corleone family won the Best Picture Oscar, and the AFI recently named it the second best film in U.S. history. More importantly, it features several noteworthy wine-related scenes, starting with the extended opening wedding sequence. Check out the scene in which Don Vito's beefy caporegime Clemenza dances an amusing jig and then demands some wine, which he promptly chugs from a pitcher. Tremendous.

Later, during a quiet transition of power, the elder Vito (Marlon Brando) reveals to son Michael (Al Pacino) his increased predilection for drinking wine, to which Michael replies: "It's good for you, pop." Amen to that.

Suggested wine pairing (for entire movie): Honor the Sicilian roots of the Corleone clan and grab a bottle of Nero d'Avola.

Suggested wine pairing (for re-enacting Clemenza dance scene): Carlo Rossi Paisano. Since much of it will likely wind up on your shirt or the floor, grab a jug of this budget-friendly table wine and get down to business.

2) *La Strada* **(1954):** Federico Fellini's breakthrough smash features a rousing scene in which Zampano (Anthony Quinn) and Gelsomina (Giulietta Masina) commemorate a successful day at the circus by drinking copious amounts of red wine. The film's powerful, wine-soaked final scene is also a classic.

Suggested wine pairing: For this celebration of circus performers, you don't want something too fussy, so opt for a nice Chianti.

3) *Mid-August Lunch* (2007): One of the best Italian comedies of the last decade or two, this pic stars Gianni Di Gregorio as a down-on-his-luck, middle-aged chap who finds himself in charge of the care and feeding of four octogenarians during a memorable 24-hour period.

Di Gregorio, who also wrote and directed, dedicates plenty of screen time to preparation of his *filetti di persico con patate* ("perch fillets with potatoes") and *pasta al forno* ("pasta bake"), and the film's humor is as deliciously dry as the white wine Di Gregorio nearly always has in hand.

Suggested wine pairing: Di Gregorio proposes pairing his signature dishes with either a Pigato (from Liguria), a Ribolla Gialla (from Friuli) or a Sagrantino di Montefalco (from Umbria). Who are we to argue?

4) *Bicycle Thieves* (1945): Many consider Vittorio De Sica's neorealist drama, which centers on a father and son in Rome desperately searching for a stolen bicycle, the greatest Italian film of all-time. While the subject matter is somber, a poignant restaurant scene in which the two chow down on mozzarella sandwiches and enjoy a carafe of wine is worth raising a glass to.

Suggested wine pairing: Go with something unpretentious but tasty, such as a Montepulciano from neighboring Abruzzo.

CHAPTER 12: THE SWEET LIFE: ITALIAN WINE AND MOVIES

5) *Big Night* (1996): Italian food has never looked so good on the big screen as in this winning comedy about two Italian brothers (Tony Shalhoub and Stanley Tucci, who also co-directed) in New Jersey, circa 1950, trying to get their Italian restaurant over the hump. Amidst the arguments over such essential questions as whether spaghetti should ever, EVER, be served as a side with risotto, generous amounts of wine are consumed.

Suggested wine pairing: A film that celebrates food so generously deserves a food-friendly wine pairing. How about a nice Brunello?

6) *The Story of Boys and Girls* (1989): Food, love and celebration. Pupi Avati's ensemble period piece about families and friends meeting to commemorate an engagement features a 20-course meal. Naturally, the wine flows freely — as do the family secrets and romantic flirtations. Avati's pic won the 1990 David di Donatello (Italian Oscar) Award for Best Film.

Suggested wine pairing: The story is set in the Tuscan hills, so sipping a wine from the region seems appropriate. Perhaps a Vino Nobile di Montepulciano?

7) *La Dolce Vita* (1960): Fellini's depiction of the sweet life a-la '60s era Rome, with journalist Marcello Rubini (Mastroianni) as our guide to the city's nightlife, is as good as cinema gets. Look for the scene early on in which Marcello asks a waiter what type of wine a celebrity a few tables over is drinking. The waiter says Soave, but a nearby patron corrects him – it's a Valpolicella. From there, indulge.

Suggested wine pairing: Keep it simple and go with, well, a Valpolicella or Soave, depending on whether you're in the mood for a red or white wine. Pairing it with snails, as the celeb does in the aforementioned scene, is strictly optional.

8) *Voyage to Italy* **(1954):** Acclaimed neorealist director Roberto Rossellini (*Rome, Open City*) married Hollywood legend Ingrid Bergman (*Casablanca*) in 1950. Together, they made five films, and the dysfunctional marriage drama *Voyage to Italy*, about a husband (George Sanders) and wife (Bergman) bickering on a jaunt to Naples, may be the best of the bunch.

Though the overall tone is serious, there is plenty of humor in *Voyage to Italy*. In one entertaining scene, Alex (Sanders) marvels at the local wine, polishes off his pitcher and goes to search for another, leading to an amusing exchange with the cleaning crew.

Suggested wine pairing: Rossellini's film showcases the cultural and natural marvels of the Naples area – museums, hot springs, dormant volcanoes and more. Pay further homage to the Campania region and pop a bottle of Falanghina or Aglianico.

9) *Yesterday, Today and Tomorrow* **(1963):** This breezy three-segment comedy from De Sica won the Academy Award for Best Foreign Language Film. In the first installment, Marcello Mastroianni and Sophia Loren celebrate outwitting the authorities – or so they think – with some wine.

Suggested wine pairing: You want something light and fizzy like the film, so consider a bottle of Prosecco or Moscato.

10) *The Godfather Part II* **(1974):** We start and end our list with the Corleone family, here saluting the greatest sequel of all-time (*Cent'anni!*). Though the tone is darker than the first film, a celebratory scene in which a young Don Vito (Robert De Niro) returns to Sicily and toasts his friends and family amidst the wine barrels marks the perfect occasion to raise your glass.

Suggested wine pairing: The greatest movie sequel of all-time deserves a wine to match. Crack a Barolo for this viewing.

10 MORE ITALIAN MOVIES THAT HAVE NOTHING TO DO WITH WINE, BUT ARE STILL PERFECT FOR VIEWING WITH A TASTY BOTTLE OF VINO

1) *Big Deal on Madonna Street* (Mario Monicelli, 1958)

2) *L'Avventura* (Michelangelo Antonioni, 1960)

3) *8-1/2* (Fellini, 1962)

4) *The Good, the Bad and the Ugly* (Leone, 1966)

5) *Deep Red* (Dario Argento, 1975)

6) *Cinema Paradiso* (Giuseppe Tornatore, 1988)

7) *Il Postino* (Michael Radford, 1994)

8) *Bread and Tulips* (Silvio Soldini, 2000)

9) *The Best of Youth* (Marco Tullio Giordana, 2003)

10) *The Great Beauty* (Paolo Sorrentino, 2014)

For more on Italian movies, please visit Ryan's website, VivaItalianMovies.com.

FAST FACT

The Sicilian winery Donnafugata makes a wine called Tancredi that's a blend of Cabernet Sauvignon and Nero d'Avola. It's inspired by the character of the same name (played by Alain Delon) in Luchino Visconti's lush period drama *The Leopard*, based on Giuseppe Tomasi di Lampedusa's best-selling book. According to the Donnafugata site, "this wine reflects the elegance and ambition of that revolutionary."

CHAPTER 13:
LA CONCLUSIONE

Now that you've reached the end of this book, you should be fully capable of sniffing out a 1998 Barolo, speaking fluent Italian, and whipping up a nice Timpano without batting an eye.

OK, so maybe you can't do any of these things quite yet. But you've come a long way in your knowledge of Italian wines. Yet while your palate may have matured like a fine Amarone, your wine journey is still just beginning.

As we've mentioned throughout this book, Italian wine is a huge landscape with numerous grape varietals, regions, styles and winemaking practices that combine to deliver the wines we're lucky enough to enjoy. Our hope is that as you worked your way through this book, this world seemed a little less intimidating every time you turned a page.

So where do you go from here? Here are a few ideas:

1) DIG DEEPER INTO THE ITALIAN WINE REGIONS.

We've emphasized that learning about Italian wine is a geographic study more than anything else. And within the confines of this introductory guide, we've covered seven of the 20 wine regions in Italy, focusing on the key varietals within those regions (and a few others). The good

CHAPTER 13: LA CONCLUSIONE

news is that this leaves 13 other regions and dozens of other wines for you to explore.

As you're venturing into ever more obscure locales and varietals, remember to Google the region your bottle comes from and note how it tasted to you. This is the best secret for building your familiarity with a broad range of Italian wines, and the exercise will help you commit these areas to memory.

At the risk of sounding like Jimmy Two Times in *Goodfellas*, we'd like to emphasize again the importance of trying new wines and discovering the ones you like best, even if some guy in a magazine (or even us in this book) told you otherwise. Wine is a personal endeavor and everyone is different in their palates, likes and dislikes; in their beliefs about what pairs with what; and in their feelings about how certain wines touch them in certain settings.

There's no absolute wrong or right. The only fair requirement is that you taste a wide variety of wines and educate yourself on their similarities and differences, their unique characteristics, and why they taste the way they do. Build a large base of knowledge to pull from, and the wine world you create for yourself will be even more fulfilling.

2) MAKE FOOD A PART OF YOUR JOURNEY.

Since it's an integral part of the Italian wine experience, we tried to provide a glimpse into the essence, brilliance and purity of Italian cuisine. In a world in which it seems like we're constantly being pressured to eat as quickly as possible with little attention to what we're consuming, traditional Italian eating customs provide a refreshing reminder that the dining experience can be about more than just shoving food in your mouth to solve a desire for nourishment.

Grant you, we'd never preach about the proper way to chow down. Ryan did, after all, infamously attempt to eat a 29-inch pizza within an hour as part of a collegiate wager. But we do encourage you to try a different approach to mealtime when you're enjoying future bottles of vino.

And while we're talking Italian food and wine, allow us to let you in on a little secret: One of the great simple pleasures in life is preparing a meal with a glass of wine in hand. And there's more good news: There are a wealth of basic Italian dishes and foods you can cook up with a minimum of culinary experience, so you don't have to be Giada De Laurentiis to get rolling in this area (though we do recommend her cookbook *Everyday Italian* as a solid kick-starter).

But regardless of whether you're whipping up a little marinara at home or eating out at your favorite restaurant, figuring out what wine to drink with which food can be perplexing. That's why we've included an appendix on suggested wine and food pairings following this chapter.

It's only a guide to get you started, but hopefully it will help you experience how wine makes food better, and vice versa. The pairing of the two is always the subject of vigorous discussion among wine and culinary professionals, and the debate will no doubt live on, because there's no guiding light showing an exact path. It's an open field, ripe for exploration with plenty of rewards along the way.

3) IMMERSE YOURSELF IN ITALIAN CULTURE.

Painting, literature, film, music. Throughout history, Italians have had a massive global impact on the arts. As you can tell, we're huge fans of the Italian entertainment and pop culture scene, and we encourage you to learn more about whatever areas of Italian art and culture most intrigue you.

Admittedly, some areas are more conducive to others when it comes to pairing with wine. Popping on some Italian music, for example, can help create a fantastic backdrop to an Italian meal paired with the perfect wine. And there are a plenty of choices to match your musical tastes, from classical (pianist Ludovico Einaudi) and opera (Luciano Pavarotti) to hip-hop (Jovanotti) and rock (Afterhours).

We're partial to Italian cinema, which is why we dedicated a chapter to the topic. There's nothing like Italian movies to serve as a window into Italian culture, where cuisine and wine mix with good company (and characters) to create good times, along with many memorable film scenes. (Check out Ryan's website VivaItalianMovies.com for more on the topic.)

Regardless of what area you delve into, it's likely you'll discover new links between Italian wine and popular culture. When you're looking for it, you'll see them more and more, and this can be a fun way to enhance your enjoyment of Italian wine.

4) BOOK THAT FLIGHT.

In writing this text, we decided we need to plan another trip to Italy soon, and we hope you'll consider visiting the country too. Being on the ground and living everything we're talking about day in and day out for a week or so can really bring enlightenment and context to the wine discussion.

If you go, please let us know about any wines, varietals or regions you found to be interesting. We're on a constant quest to build knowledge about all those small wine-producing pockets of Italy we know are kicking out fantastic wines that don't see distribution beyond the city where they're produced. Speaking of which, if you find some of these, you might want to stuff a few bottles in your suitcase — it will be the best money you've ever spent on a checked bag fee.

5) LOOK BEYOND ITALY.

It may seem blasphemous in a book about Italian wine, but since we're at the end of this guide there's something we have to admit: There are some really incredible wines outside of Italy. And if the Italian wine world seems large, imagine the size of the global wine industry. France, Spain, South America, Portugal, Australia and others produce many world-class wines that rank with the best of the best.

How to tackle this massive global wine world? Consider taking a cue from this book, in which we focused on the most common Italian wines and regions. The same approach can be applied to other countries' wine regions to help bolster your overall wine education. When you enjoy a bottle from France, look at the label, find the region, Google a map of it, find out what varietals are produced there, check the vintage … do all the things we've talked about in *Decoding Italian Wine*.

And if you're looking for a guide to help you explore the wine world outside of Italy's borders, Andrew has you covered. Check out his previous books, *Decoding French Wine* and *Around the Wine World in 40 Pages*.

When you start down the path, you'll quickly learn that wine exploration is a lifelong journey and one that's made more complex (and interesting) every time a new vintage enters the world. You'll also learn that this is exactly why we love it. It's an evolving game that never ends and only gets better. We can't think of anything else in the world quite like it, so we hope you'll join in. *Buona fortuna!*

APPENDIX I:
ITALIAN WINE AND FOOD PAIRING GUIDE

"A bottle of red, a bottle of white.
It all depends on your appetite."

— Billy Joel, "Scenes from an Italian Restaurant"

Learning how to best pair Italian food and wine is a journey much like drinking vino: deeply personal, highly subjective and requiring (thoroughly enjoyable) trial and error.

The basic approach is to pair red wines with hearty red sauces and red meats, while opting for white wines for lighter sauces, fish and chicken. The idea is that you want to pick a strong, earthy wine that can stand up to a powerful dish without being overwhelmed by it as a lighter wine would. Similarly, pairing a lighter wine with a lighter dish can bring out the best in each.

To take it up a notch, try selecting a wine from the same region as the dish you're preparing. For example, a fish recipe from Northern Italy might take a Soave, while something from Tuscany could be paired with a Brunello.

Bearing in mind that Italian cuisine is rich and varied and could take up an entire book on its own, here's a sampling of more than 20 common dishes and potential wine pairings:

Food	Suggested Wine Pairing
Meat and cheese antipasto	Dolcetto
Fried calamari	Prosecco or Falanghina
Prosciutto and melone (e.g., cantaloupe)	Pinot Grigio or Orvieto
Prosciutto and mozzarella panini	Chianti
Beef and cheese manicotti	Nero d'Avola
Spaghetti all'amatriciana	Montepulciano d'Abruzzo
Linguine with Bolognese sauce	Valpolicella
Rigatoni with vodka sauce	Chianti
Gnocchi with pesto	Gavi
Wild mushroom ravioli with mushroom sauce	Soave
Butternut squash ravioli with brown butter sauce	Arneis
Mushroom risotto	Barolo or Barbaresco
Seafood risotto	Greco di Tufo
Lasagna	Chianti or other Sangiovese
Pizza	Chianti, Aglianico, Coda di Volpe (depending on topping)
Eggplant parmigiana	Aglianico
Chicken piccata	Soave
Chicken saltimbocca	Arneis

Veal marsala .... Nero d'Avola

Braised short ribs .... Amarone

Steak Florentine.. Brunello or Super Tuscan

Osso buco .... Vino Nobile di Montepulciano

Cannoli .... Marsala

Tiramisu .... Moscato

That should get the party started. As your wine journey continues, get bolder and try new and unorthodox pairings. You'll come across some unexpected gems and have a lot of fun in the process.

APPENDIX II:
ITALIAN WINE-RELATED PHRASES

Whether you're sipping wine in a small Italian *ristorante* or just hanging out with friends and enjoying some vino, it's fun to sprinkle some Italian phrases into the conversation.

Here's a list of some Italian wine-related words and sentences we think will enhance your wine-drinking adventures – some polite, some festive and others humorous:

Italian Phrase	English Translation
Cin cin / Salute	Cheers
Cent'anni	A hundred years of good luck
Cento di questi giorni	May you live a hundred years
Vorrei un bicchiere di vino rosso	I would like a glass of red wine
Vorremmo un litro di vino bianco della casa, per favore	We would like a liter of the house wine, please
Un mezzo litro di questo vino, per favore	A half-liter of this wine, please
Posso avere un po' di vino, per favore?	May I have a little wine, please?
Vino della zona	Wine produced nearby
Piu, per favore	More, please

APPENDIX II: ITALIAN WINE-RELATED PHRASES

Un'altra, per favore.. Another, please

Un'altra bottiglia di vino,   Another bottle of wine,

per favore .... please

Questo vino è delizioso .... This wine is delicious

Questo vino è molto brutto .... This wine is very bad

Il conto, per favore... The check, please

Io sono stanco .... I'm tired

Io bevuto troppo .... I drank too much

Non puoi avere la botte

piena e la moglie ubriaca .... You can't have a full wine
                                                   barrel and a drunk wife
                                                   (i.e., you can't have your cake
                                                   and eat it too)

APPENDIX III:
THE TOP 10 BEST-SELLING ITALIAN WINES OF 2013 AT WINE.COM

1) Ruffino Modus 2009
   50% Sangiovese, 25% Cabernet Sauvignon, 25% Merlot
   Tuscany, Italy
   $27.99
   #14 overall

2) Antinori Villa Toscana 2009
   Sangiovese, Cabernet Sauvignon, Merlot, Syrah
   Tuscany, Italy
   $25
   #19 overall

3) La Marco Prosecco
   Glera
   Veneto, Italy
   $17
   #20 overall

4) Fattoria del Cerro Vino Nobile di Montepulciano 2009
   Sangiovese
   Tuscany, Italy
   $25
   #56 overall

5) Bibi Graetz Casamatta Rosso 2011
Sangiovese
Tuscany, Italy
$13.99
#59 overall

6) Falesco Merlot
Merlot
Umbria, Italy
$18
#61 overall

7) Da Vinci Riserva Chianti 2007
Sangiovese
Tuscany, Italy
$25
#64 overall

8) Santa Margherita Pinot Grigio
Pinot Grigio
Trentino-Alto Adige, Italy
$19.99
#69 overall

9) Antinori Tignanello 2009
80% Sangiovese, 15% Cabernet Sauvignon, 5% Cabernet Franc
Tuscany, Italy
$105
#73 overall

10) Tenute Silvio Nardi Brunello di Montalcino 2007
Sangiovese
Tuscany, Italy
$74.99
#78 overall

ACKNOWLEDGEMENTS

Andrew would like to thank his wife Amy first and foremost for tending to a newborn child during much of the writing of this book while I bunkered up in the basement with a bottle of Brunello typing away late into the night. In addition to those duties, she also served as a key editor for my sometimes-jumbled (Brunello-influenced) writing.

I'd also like to thank my brother Tyler for his seemingly unlimited wine budget that has helped me acquire, taste and appreciate many of the excellent Italian wines I've enjoyed in my life. And lastly, I'd like to thank my parents Richard and Carol Cullen who reviewed multiple drafts of this manuscript and made many valuable suggestions for making it better.

Ryan would like to thank his wife Vanessa for joining me on this wine journey and supporting me during the writing process, and my children Marisa and Daniela for regularly making me laugh — and occasionally allowing me a few minutes to write. In addition, I'd like to express my gratitude to my parents Ron and Rosemarie McNally for mixing my first "wine and water" and encouraging me to study abroad in Italy.

The only thing better than enjoying good food and drink is sharing it with good company, so I'd also like to thank my family members who have joined me for many Italian meals and bottles of wine over the years, including Erin McNally and Clark Henry, A.J. and Allison Rollins, Luther and Emily Christofoli, Sandy Moglia and Tim Chung, Camille Moglia-D'Onofrio and Joseph Fratta Jr. *Grazie!*

ABOUT THE AUTHORS

Andrew Cullen is the author of *Decoding French Wine: A Beginner's Guide to Enjoying the Fruits of the French Terroir* and *Around the Wine World in 40 Pages: An Exploration Guide for the Beginning Wine Enthusiast.* He is a digital marketer for a global 100 brand and the founder and editor of several websites including CostcoWineBlog.com and ToysBulletin.com.

Ryan McNally is the creator of VivaItalianMovies.com and the author of *Class Dismissed: 75 Outrageous, Mind-Expanding College Exploits.* He is the manager of content marketing for a leading digital marketing software company and has written for dozens of magazines and websites on topics including music, sports and film.

Made in the USA
Middletown, DE
20 December 2019